AS Economics
UNIT 2

Edexcel

Unit 2: Markets — Why They Fail

Mark Gavin

Philip Allan Updates
Market Place
Deddington
Oxfordshire
OX15 0SE

tel: 01869 338652
fax: 01869 337590
e-mail: sales@philipallan.co.uk
www.philipallan.co.uk

© Philip Allan Updates 2003

ISBN-13: 978-0-86003-682-1
ISBN-10: 0-86003-682-0

This Guide has been written specifically to support students preparing for the Edexcel AS Economics Unit 2 examination. The content has been neither approved nor endorsed by Edexcel and remains the sole responsibility of the author.

Printed by Information Press, Eynsham, Oxford

Contents

Introduction

Aims 4

How to use this guide 4

Exam format 5

Assessment objectives 5

Planning your revision: general points 6

A 4-week structured revision plan 7

How to answer data-response questions 8

Checklist of revision questions 11

Grade descriptions 13

■ ■ ■

Content Guidance

About this section 16

Market failure 17

Types of market failure 21

Remedies for market failure 34

Government failure 47

■ ■ ■

Questions and Answers

About this section 56

Q1 Postal services in the UK 57

Q2 The UK tobacco market 63

Q3 The North Sea fishing industry 69

Q4 Terminal 5: Heathrow Airport 74

Q5 UK health-care provision 80

Q6 The Common Agricultural Policy (CAP) 85

Introduction

Aims

This guide has been written to prepare students for Unit 2 of Edexcel's Advanced Subsidiary (AS) GCE examination in economics. It provides an overview of the knowledge and skills required to achieve a high grade in the examination for 'Markets — Why They Fail'. This unit considers the nature of market failure, its causes and possible remedies. It examines why markets might not allocate resources efficiently and methods of dealing with market failure, together with an evaluation of their effectiveness. It also considers how government intervention may create market failure. 'Markets — Why They Fail' can be broken down into four broad topics that cover the unit specification shown below.

(1) Market failure: allocative and productive efficiency; economies of scale; long-run and short-run average costs.

(2) Types of market failure: monopoly; public goods and quasi-public goods; merit and demerit goods; external costs and benefits.

(3) Remedies for market failure: for monopoly — regulation and promotion of market entry; for external costs and demerit goods — direct controls, prohibition, tradable permits, extension of property rights, environmental taxes; for public goods, merit goods and external benefits — government provision and subsidies.

(4) Government failure: lack of market information; the distortion of market forces; conflicts in government objectives; regulatory capture; time-lag in decision-making.

How to use this guide

This guide provides a summary of the knowledge and skills required to achieve a high grade in Unit 2. It also focuses on exam techniques, including typical questions and answers and what the examiners are looking for. It should ideally be used as a supplement to a taught course and with textbooks and other materials recommended by your teacher.

This introduction explains the examination format and the skills that will be tested. It also provides useful tips on revision planning and sitting the examination. A revision programme for the 4-week period before the Unit 2 examination is included.

The Content Guidance section provides an overview of the topics, identifying what has to be learnt and explaining key economic concepts and models. Typical examination mistakes made by students are also shown, plus links that exist between topics. These are favourite areas for the examiner to set questions on.

The final part of the guide provides questions and answers on the economic concepts and topics in Unit 2. There are six data-response questions covering relevant topics, with a selection of student answers ranging in quality from grade A to grade C. The examiner's comments that accompany these answers give an insight into how marks are awarded and what pitfalls should be avoided.

Exam format

Unit 2 makes up 30% of the weighting for the AS examination (and 15% for the A-level). In the examination candidates are required to answer one data-response question from a choice of two.

The amount of time allowed for the examination is 1 hour and there is a maximum of 40 marks available. Each data-response question will usually be divided into four parts: (a), (b), (c) and (d); sometimes these may be subdivided into two further parts.

Assessment objectives

There are four assessment objectives, or sets of skills, in each unit of AS and A-level economics. Examiners are required to test candidates on these skills, and the exam papers are devised specifically to integrate them into questions.

It is useful to bear in mind what these assessment objectives are. Each objective is given a weight to show its relative importance. In 'Markets — Why They Fail,' assessment objectives 1 and 2 have a higher weighting than objectives 3 and 4, as shown in the table below.

Objective	Assessment objectives	Weighting
1	**Knowledge and understanding:** demonstrate knowledge and understanding of the specified content.	30%
2	**Application:** apply knowledge and critical understanding to problems and issues arising from both familiar and unfamiliar situations.	30%
3	**Analysis:** analyse economic problems and issues.	20%
4	**Evaluation:** evaluate economic arguments and evidence, making informed judgements.	20%

Knowledge and understanding

This objective involves defining and comprehending important economic terms such as public goods, merit goods and demerit goods. It also refers to understanding economic models such as the price mechanism and how they may fail to allocate resources efficiently.

Application

This is the ability to select economic concepts and apply them to real-world issues such as the application of indirect taxes to tobacco and petrol markets, or the application of subsidies to public transport. It involves explaining the processes and effects.

Analysis

This means examining and breaking down an economic model or issue, e.g. the use of externalities to distinguish between the market and social optimum allocation of resources.

Evaluation

This involves assessing an economic argument or evidence that is presented. It tends to have a critical element to it, e.g. evaluating the success of tradable permits in reducing pollution, or weighing up the advantages and disadvantages of student tuition fees in higher education. Candidates are expected to offer their views and justify them.

Planning your revision: general points

Revision for AS and A-level examinations requires careful organisation and planning. There are several steps to consider:

- **Make sure you are familiar with the requirements of the unit.** You should get a copy of the specification and any past exam papers, including the relevant specimen paper. Ensure that your notes relate to the topics in the specification and questions.
- **Make sure you have all your resources in order.** Class notes should be complete and placed into topic areas. If there are any gaps in your notes, it is important to fill them as soon as possible. Your teacher could help you put notes in order to ensure there are no glaring omissions, and you should refer to at least one of the AS/A-level textbooks. Add to and refine your notes as your understanding improves.
- **Set targets to a timescale.** You should draw up a programme to revise the unit over a realistic timescale before the exams. This will involve breaking down your notes into bite-sized chunks to revise from. A thorough coverage is important because the data-response questions can be drawn from any part of the specification. A 4-week revision plan is shown on the next page.
- **Choose a suitable method of revision.** It is useful to conduct an overall sweep of your notes to ensure you understand every concept and model. After this, many students find it helpful to précis their notes onto study cards to help remember key points. This involves summarising the notes into a series of concepts, models and diagrams which act as pointers to more detailed information, as well as speeding up revision. Some students find it helpful to put their notes in a pictorial form where possible. However, spider diagrams and cartoons may not suit everyone and so it is important to select what is best for you.
- **Active revision is essential.** You should ask questions on the topics and test yourself on memory and understanding. A 'study buddy' can help here and you can also compare ideas and revision notes. Finally, your revision should include frequent practice of answering questions under timed conditions.

A 4-week structured revision plan

Hours	Week 1	Week 2	Week 3	Week 4
1st	Definition of and types of market failure; role of productive and allocative efficiency; diagrammatic explanation.	The relationship between private, external and social costs; diagrammatic explanation showing welfare loss.	The relationship between private, external and social benefits; diagrammatic explanation showing potential welfare gain.	Advantages and disadvantages of extending property rights to correct market failure.
2nd	Monopoly and types of barriers to entry; the economic effects of a monopoly on consumers and producers.	The application of indirect taxation to internalise external costs and reach social optimum position; assess the use of the tax system in this way.	The application of government subsidies to reach social optimum position; assess the use of subsidies in this way.	Advantages and disadvantages of road pricing to correct market failure.
3rd	The regulation of monopolies, e.g. limits to market share and utility regulators.	The advantages and disadvantages of tradable pollution permits to correct market failure.	Merit goods and the application to health care and education.	Government failure in markets: lack of information and distortion of market forces.
4th	Policies to promote the growth of new firms and competition.	Demerit goods and the application to tobacco consumption. Read through Question 2 from this guide.	Public goods and quasi-public goods. Read through Question 4 from this guide.	Government failure in markets: efficiency versus equity; regulatory capture; time-lags.
5th	Exam practice: Question 1 from this guide.	Exam practice: Question 3 from this guide.	Exam practice: Question 5 from this guide.	Exam practice: Question 6 from this guide.

The revision plan above is a guide to how to break down Unit 2 into manageable topics in the 4 weeks prior to the examinations (which can be taken in either January or June of the academic year). However, there is a large overlap between Units 1 and 2 of the specification and it may be useful to revise them together. This would mean condensing the plan into 2 weeks, leaving room for you to revise Unit 1: 'Markets — How They Work'. Note that the same amount of time should be spent revising Unit 1 and Unit 2, with a minimum of 20 hours study for each. The plan above focuses on Unit 2 and you should refer to the revision guide on Unit 1 to work out a more comprehensive programme.

When drawing up a revision plan, you must ensure that sufficient time is allocated to each of your subjects and then to the units within them. As you are likely to be studying four subjects in Year 12, you should aim to complete between 1 and 2 hours of revision per subject per day on those days when no school lessons are timetabled. Since there are three units in each AS subject, this does not leave much time for revising an individual unit. Revision time is at a premium and you must make sure you use it effectively. The topics in the revision plan are broken into 1-hour revision slots together with exam practice sessions.

How to answer data-response questions

In Unit 2, you have a choice between two data-response questions. It is important to read both questions before choosing which one to answer and to stick to the time limit of 1 hour. Most questions include a mixture of text and graphs or tables.

There are a number of key points to take into account when answering data-response questions, namely:

- **Identify the key economic concepts and models.** Remember that examiners select the data in order to test your knowledge of the specification content. For example, a data-response question on transport or pollution is likely to test you on external costs, whereas a data-response question on health care or education is likely to test you on external benefits (both including a diagrammatic explanation). A data-response question on a monopoly is likely to test you on types of barriers to entry and government regulation.
- **Read the instructions of questions very carefully** and focus your answers on them. A major mistake many candidates make is to ignore the instructions. The following is a list of command words and their meanings used in data-response and essay questions:

  Account for — explain something, e.g. 'account for the growth in road traffic in the UK over the past 40 years'.

  Analyse — break down and explain the meaning of an economic topic or problem. This typically involves a critical view when accompanied by '*the extent to which*', e.g. 'analyse the extent to which road pricing is an effective means of reducing traffic congestion'.

  Assess — estimate the quality or quantity of something, e.g. 'assess the arguments for and against an increase in state funding of higher education'. Acceptable answers can be substantially different in their view, providing the correct reasoning is used.

  Compare — describe two situations and present the similarities and differences between them, e.g. 'compare the use of taxes with regulations to limit motor vehicle pollution'.

  Critically examine — present a view on a contentious issue, e.g. 'critically examine the replacement of student grants with student loans in higher education'. You will need to present the merits and demerits of the topic; the word 'criticise' *does not mean* you must be hostile to the issue at hand.

Define — make clear the meaning of a term. You need to learn all the definitions of key economic concepts identified in the Content Guidance section of this guide. Often there will be a definition question on key terms, e.g. 'define market failure' or 'define government failure'.

Describe — present a detailed picture of the issue at hand, e.g. 'describe how tradable permits operate to limit pollution costs'. There is no element of criticism implied in the question and so your answer should be neutral.

Discuss — draw attention to various aspects of the question, including giving arguments for and against, e.g. 'discuss possible reasons for the growth of airport traffic in recent years'. It could involve some evaluation — explaining why some points are more important than others.

Distinguish between — point out the difference between two factors. It is likely to involve a definition of term(s), e.g. 'distinguish between private benefits and social benefits'.

Evaluate — make an appraisal of an economic issue by examining the case for and against, and then giving an opinion in the light of the evidence. It is similar to the term '**assess**'. You may find that some factors are more important than others in your answer, e.g. 'evaluate the likely effectiveness of any two measures the government could undertake to reduce the consumption of tobacco'. It may be argued that high indirect taxes are more effective than a ban on smoking in public places.

Examine — explain and analyse a particular economic issue or problem and then discuss its merits, e.g. 'examine two reasons why the public sector share of health care differs between the UK and the USA'.

Explain — make known in detail an economic term or problem and give reasons for it, e.g. 'explain how the extension of property rights to the seas might protect fish stocks'. Your answer may also include relevant examples and diagrams.

Identify — state the factors required. There is no need to offer an explanation as this wastes time. It is unlikely that there will be many marks available, e.g. 'identify two external benefits and two external costs of operating an international airport in south Yorkshire', for just 2 marks.

Outline — give the main features of a particular economic term or issue. You should pay careful attention to the marks available as they are likely to be relatively few, e.g. 'outline the case for and against an expansion in the provision of higher education in the UK through an increase in the number of private universities and colleges'. An answer to this question could be very lengthy; however, it is important to stick to the main points.

Use supply and demand analysis — include relevant diagrams in your analysis. In Unit 2 it is difficult to analyse market failure without the use of supply and demand diagrams.

What — explain briefly the meaning of an economic term or issue, e.g. 'what is meant by the term "public good"'?

With reference to the data — include points extracted from the data provided.

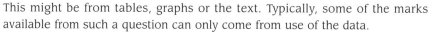

This might be from tables, graphs or the text. Typically, some of the marks available from such a question can only come from use of the data.

- **Take careful note of the units of measurement** as this is where common mistakes are made. For example, data in the form of large numbers may be shown in thousands, millions or even billions. It is also important to distinguish between 'values' (expressed in monetary terms) and 'volumes' (expressed in quantitative terms).

- **Select the relevant material.** Read all the data carefully, including headings, subheadings and sources, then select what is relevant to the answer (note that some of the material is background information and not directly relevant). Do not describe everything in minute detail or reproduce the data exactly.

- **Pay close attention to any conclusions drawn in the text** and work out the main line of argument. You need to sift through the information searching for trends and relationships and link these to the questions set.

- **Identify the general trends and sub-trends** within the data and use these in developing your answer. Examiners allocate points for the use of data and it is important to remember that part of the answer lies in the information given. Trends may be upward, downward or cyclical. For example, an upward trend is portrayed by long-term earnings growth in the UK; a downward trend is shown by government subsidies to the railway industry; and a cyclical trend can be seen in house price movements in the economy.

- **Look for relationships within the data.** There may be a direct relationship (e.g. between electricity generation and atmospheric pollution — they both increase together) or an indirect relationship (e.g. between tobacco consumption and the size of tobacco tax as shown in Question 2; it is likely the increase in tobacco taxation explains the fall in tobacco sales at least in part). Sometimes there is no apparent relationship in the data provided and so it is relevant to state this point.

- **Be prepared to manipulate data** through calculating the percentage or percentage change. Sometimes you are asked to calculate this specifically, as with tobacco sales in Question 2 and Heathrow's share of air passenger traffic in Question 4. Make sure you do not confuse variations in rates of change with variations in absolute levels (e.g. falling house price inflation is not the same as falling house prices). You should also show the working of calculations because if you get the wrong answer due to a numerical mistake, some credit may still be given for using the correct method.

- **Start your answer by explaining simple economic concepts and arguments** that apply to the question. Later, you can gradually develop more sophisticated ideas if appropriate. This means that you will gain marks even if you go on to make errors in the answer.

- **Extend your answer beyond the confines of the data.** It is often a good idea to think of what other data you would like to have to answer the question. Data-response papers sometimes include a question on what further information would be useful for you to make a more effective evaluation. Practise thinking about this additional data when attempting the exercises.

- **Be aware of limitations and bias within the data** and the origins of the article. For example, it could be a trade union or employers' federation report. Sometimes articles from pressure groups are used and you must remember that they may have been written by economists at different ends of the political spectrum. It is often the case that more than one answer can be correct since economics is full of controversy and disagreement.
- **Stick to the time allocation:** 1 hour in total. Edexcel advises you to spend the first 5 minutes reading the paper and choosing which data-response question to answer. You should also leave 5 minutes to check your work at the end, making any necessary alterations to your answers. This leaves 50 minutes to earn the 40 marks available. Most data-response questions are open-ended and so it is impossible to cover every angle in your answer. You should consider the marks available for each question and allocate your time accordingly. Questions worth 2 or 3 marks should be answered within about 4 minutes, whereas a 10-mark question should be given approximately 12 minutes.
- **Keep up to date.** Economics is a discipline which tries to make sense of the real world and you are expected to know what is going on in the economy. It is important that you are aware of topical issues since the exam questions are based on these. You should make an effort to read a quality newspaper regularly, watch the television news and subscribe to relevant magazines such as *Economic Review*.
- **Be aware of the general trends in the topics stated in the specification,** for example: road congestion; public transport provision; environmental pollution; tradable permits; extension of property rights; waste disposal; tourism; health care; the provision of education; and agricultural stabilisation policies. You need to be familiar with the general trends surrounding these topics whilst bearing in mind that memorising whole series of statistical data is a waste of time. For example, with reference to road congestion, it is pertinent to consider the reasons for the growth in motor vehicle use in the UK and policies which might reduce this growth; with regard to agricultural stabilisation policies, it is useful to know the reasons for government intervention, the form it takes and why there are efforts to reduce the size of the subsidies.

Checklist of revision questions

The following questions will help you to break down your revision into manageable topic areas. You should be able to answer them all before you take the examination.

Market failure: monopoly

(1) Define market failure and identify the main types.
(2) Explain what is meant by a monopoly and list its characteristics.
(3) Explain the types of barriers to entry to an industry that a firm might face.
(4) What barriers to exit might exist for firms?
(5) Distinguish between total costs, average costs and marginal costs; show the formula for each.

(6) What is the difference between short-run and long-run costs?

(7) Define economies of scale and list the different types.

(8) What are the likely economic disadvantages of a monopoly?

(9) What are the possible economic advantages of a monopoly?

(10) How does the government regulate monopolies? You should refer to the Competition Commission and the utility regulators.

Market failure: public, merit and demerit goods

(1) Using examples, distinguish between a public good and a private good.

(2) Using examples, distinguish between a merit good and a demerit good.

(3) The government recently announced a major programme of increased expenditure on the National Health Service (from £51 billion in the year 2000 to £68 billion by the year 2004). What factors may have caused the government to increase spending in this area by so much?

(4) Make a list of the advantages and disadvantages of government provision of health care in the UK.

(5) Why is there a shortage of doctors and nurses in the National Health Service?

(6) What economic arguments exist for the expansion of private health care in the UK?

(7) List the advantages and disadvantages of replacing student grants with loans in higher education.

(8) Why is education considered to be a merit good?

(9) Why is there a shortage of school teachers in certain subjects, for example, languages, science and maths?

(10) What measures could the government take to reduce the teaching shortage?

Market failure: externalities

(1) Define the term 'externality'.

(2) Explain the relationship between private costs, external costs and social costs.

(3) Explain the relationship between private benefits, external benefits and social benefits.

(4) (a) Construct a diagram to show the external costs in the production of a chemical.

    (b) Identify the free market price and quantity and the social optimum price and quantity.

    (c) Shade in the area of welfare loss.

(5) (a) Construct a diagram to show the external benefits in the consumption of vaccinations.

    (b) Identify the free market price and quantity and the social optimum price and quantity.

    (c) Shade in the area of potential welfare gain.

(6) Make a list of all the external costs involved in the construction and use of a motorway.

Market failure: remedies

(1) What are tradable pollution permits?

(2) List the advantages and disadvantages of tradable permits as a means of controlling pollution in the electricity power generation industry.

(3) Explain the meaning of road pricing.

(4) List the advantages and disadvantages of road pricing as a means of reducing road traffic congestion.

(5) Construct a diagram to show the application of an indirect tax on petrol to control motor vehicle pollution.

(6) List the advantages and disadvantages of indirect taxation as a means of reducing pollution.

(7) Explain the term 'extension of property rights'.

(8) List the advantages and disadvantages of extending property rights to the seas to protect fish stocks.

(9) Make a list of government regulations which have the effect of reducing motor vehicle pollution.

(10) Construct a diagram to show the application of a subsidy to public transport.

(11) List the advantages and disadvantages of government subsidies to promote the use of public transport.

Government failure

(1) Define 'government failure' and identify the main types.

(2) Construct a diagram to show how the application of a minimum wage might cause unemployment in a labour market.

(3) Construct a diagram to show how the application of a maximum rent might cause a shortage of rental accommodation.

(4) Construct a diagram to show how the application of a guaranteed minimum price for agricultural products might cause a surplus.

(5) What costs are involved with the European food surpluses?

(6) Why might government subsidies lead to economic inefficiency?

(7) Draw a buffer stock diagram.

(8) Why do buffer stock policies tend to break down?

(9) Make a list of the advantages and disadvantages of the National Minimum Wage.

Grade descriptions

Edexcel provides grade descriptions for examiners to use as a guide to their marking. The grade awarded will depend upon the extent to which the candidate has met the overall assessment objectives. Shortcomings in some aspects of the exam may be balanced by better performances elsewhere.

Grade A

Candidates will demonstrate in-depth knowledge and critical understanding of a wide range of economic theories and concepts. They will apply this knowledge and understanding to analyse familiar and unfamiliar situations, issues and problems using appropriate numerical and non-numerical techniques accurately. They will evaluate

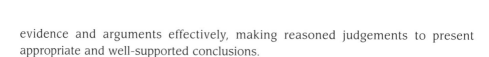

evidence and arguments effectively, making reasoned judgements to present appropriate and well-supported conclusions.

Grade C

Candidates will demonstrate knowledge and understanding of a range of economic theories and concepts. They will apply this knowledge and understanding to analyse familiar and unfamiliar situations, issues and problems using appropriate numerical and non-numerical techniques. They will evaluate evidence and arguments to present reasoned conclusions.

Grade E

Candidates will demonstrate knowledge and understanding of a limited range of economic theories and concepts. They will show some ability to use this knowledge and understanding in order to analyse familiar and unfamiliar situations, issues and problems making use of numerical and non-numerical techniques. Candidates' evaluation of evidence and arguments will be limited.

Content
Guidance

Economics consists of two broad areas of study: **microeconomics** and **macro-economics**. Microeconomics is the study of individual markets within the economy and this is covered in Units 1 and 2 of the Edexcel AS specification ('Markets — How They Work' and 'Markets — Why They Fail'). Macroeconomics looks at how the economy functions as a whole, and this is covered in Unit 3 of the specification ('Managing the Economy').

This section focuses on essential information, including economic concepts and models that students need to understand for Unit 2: Markets — Why They Fail. These are explained under the following headings:

- Market failure (p. 17)
- Types of market failure (p. 21)
- Remedies for market failure (p. 34)
- Government failure (p. 47)

Market failure

Essential information

All economies experience market failure. This occurs when the price mechanism fails to deliver economic efficiency and resources are not allocated to their optimum use. Economic efficiency has two components: allocative and productive efficiency.

Allocative efficiency

This is where a firm produces the quantity of goods and services consumers want at a price they are prepared to pay. Allocative efficiency occurs when the cost to a firm of producing the last unit of a good equals the benefit obtained by the consumer, i.e. the marginal cost of producing a good is equated with the marginal benefit from consuming it.

To measure the benefit or utility consumers gain from a good, economists use the 'price' consumers are prepared to pay for it. For example, an individual who is prepared to pay £80 for a pair of trainers is assumed to gain £80 of benefit from them. It might not be a perfect measure of consumer benefit but it is generally regarded as the best available.

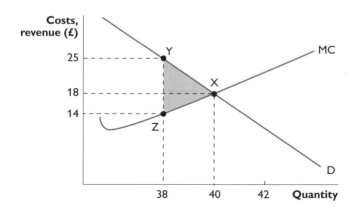

Figure 1 Allocative efficiency in production

Figure 1 shows the marginal cost and demand curves for a firm. Allocative efficiency is at an output level of 40 units and a price of £18 per unit. This is where the marginal cost of the 40th unit of output to the firm equals the benefit obtained by the consumer of that last unit of output at £18.

Allocative inefficiency occurs if output is above or below 40 units. At an output of 38, the benefit from consuming the last unit (£25) exceeds the cost of producing it (£14). It is possible to raise overall welfare by increasing output. The welfare gained is shown by the triangle XYZ. At an output of 42, the benefit from consuming the last unit is less than the cost of producing it. It is possible to raise overall welfare by decreasing output.

Allocative efficiency is concerned with matching consumer benefit with producer cost for the last unit of a good.

Productive efficiency

This is where a firm produces a good or service at minimum average cost. It means that the cost per unit of output is minimised and indicates that the firm is utilising all its resources fully. The firm is producing at its full capacity level. Productive efficiency is also known as the optimum output level. Table 1 shows the total, average and marginal costs of production of a good for a firm. Note the optimum output is where average costs are minimised. This is also the output where marginal costs intersect average costs as shown in Figure 2.

Table 1 Costs of production for a firm

Total output	Total cost (£)	Marginal cost (£)	Average cost (£)
0	50,000	–	–
1	90,000	40,000	90,000
2	120,000	30,000	60,000
3	150,000	30,000	50,000
4	190,000	40,000	47,500
5	260,000	50,000	52,000
6	320,000	60,000	53,333
7	410,000	70,000	58,600
8	510,000	100,000	63,800

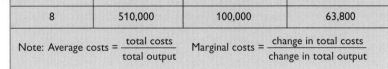

Note: Average costs = $\dfrac{\text{total costs}}{\text{total output}}$ Marginal costs = $\dfrac{\text{change in total costs}}{\text{change in total output}}$

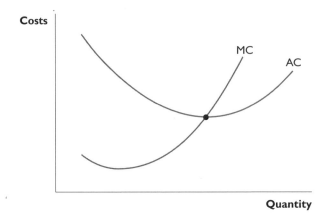

Figure 2 Productive efficiency

Summary

Market failure occurs when economic efficiency is not achieved. For an individual firm this means its average costs are above the minimum possible (productive inefficiency) or the cost of producing the last unit is not equated with the benefit obtained from its consumption (allocative inefficiency).

Economies of scale

Economies of scale refer to the advantages of large-scale production. Long-run average costs fall as production increases. An economy of scale occurs where output increases more than in proportion to inputs — this is also known as increasing returns to scale. **Internal economies of scale** occur within the firm as it expands production. **External economies of scale** are achieved as the industry grows and they benefit all firms within it.

Types of internal economies of scale

- **Financial:** a large firm tends to be well known and finds it easier to raise finance at favourable rates of interest. Some large firms are quoted on the stock exchange and are able to issue new shares when they require funds.
- **Managerial:** a large firm can employ specialist managers. For example, Ford Motor Company has its own department of lawyers, accountants, research engineers and linguists. Managers in a large firm can also supervise greater numbers of staff, leading to lower managerial costs per unit of output.
- **Marketing:** a large firm can spread its advertising costs over a greater volume of sales and so gain lower costs per unit. For example, large firms may advertise on national television and in national newspapers; although the lump sum cost of these adverts is high, the cost per unit of sales ends up being quite low because of the high volume of sales made.
- **Purchasing:** a large firm can buy raw materials and components in big quantities and gain discounts from its suppliers. For example, supermarkets can drive down the price of fruit and vegetables purchased from farmers because of the large volumes involved.
- **Research and development:** a large firm can afford big research projects which are often out of reach of small firms. In the pharmaceutical industry a handful of giant firms dominate the drugs market because of their ability to invest heavily in research and development.
- **Risk-bearing:** a large firm can undertake more investments and spread its risks by expanding into different markets. A good example is Virgin, a firm involved in music production, air travel, rail travel, cosmetics, soft drinks, clothing and financial services.
- **Technical:** a large firm typically uses bigger scale machinery and factories than a small firm, driving down the unit costs of production. For example, an oil tanker which is twice the size of another tanker has eight times the volume. The unit cost of transporting oil falls as the size of tanker increases.

Types of external economies of scale

- **Labour:** a pool of skilled labour develops in an area where similar firms might concentrate. Examples include the footwear industry in Northampton and furniture-making in High Wycombe.
- **Ancillary services:** these develop to support an industry. One example is the textile industry in Oldham, which is supported by college courses, specialist manufacturers and repairers of textile machinery.
- **Cooperation:** this may arise between firms in the same industry. For example, grocery stores may join organisations which conduct advertising and bulk buying for them, such as Mace and Spar.

Internal economies of scale occur within a firm as it expands production and moves down the average cost curve.

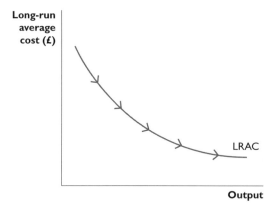

Figure 3 Internal economies of scale

External economies of scale shift the average cost curve downwards at each output level.

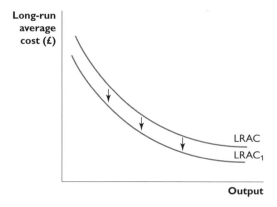

Figure 4 External economies of scale

The distinction between the short-run and long-run average cost curve

The short-run average cost curve is U-shaped because of the law of diminishing returns. This is where successive units of a variable factor input are added to a set of fixed factor inputs, eventually causing total output to rise at a diminishing rate. The slowdown in the growth of output pushes up the average costs of production.

However, the law of diminishing returns does not apply to long-run cost curves because all factor inputs are assumed to be variable. Long-run average costs may rise due to diseconomies of scale setting into the production process. These occur when firms become too large and suffer from poor coordination or poor staff morale.

Figure 5 shows the relationship between short-run and long-run average cost curves for a firm. Each short-run cost curve represents a potential plant size that a firm can reach. By drawing the envelope to these curves, the long-run average cost curve is derived.

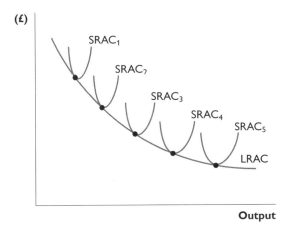

Figure 5 Short-run and long-run average cost curves

Types of market failure

Monopoly formation

A free market has several characteristics which promote competition and economic efficiency:
- a large number of buyers and sellers acting independently of each other
- free entry and exit for firms to the market
- both firms and consumers have good market knowledge
- each firm has only a small market share and so cannot influence market price

In these circumstances firms may achieve allocative and productive efficiency.

However, in some markets there is a lack of competition — this results in market failure. In such markets:
- a few large firms dominate production
- there are high entry and exit barriers
- there is poor market knowledge
- competition is limited
- in extreme cases monopolies may form

Monopolies are more concerned with making profits or increasing market share than achieving economic efficiency. It is unlikely that monopolies will achieve allocative and productive efficiency and so the markets fail.

A **pure monopoly** is where a firm has 100% market share. In effect, the firm is the industry. Examples include the regional water companies which supply water services to households within each region. They have no direct competition within their own regions.

However, it is possible for a firm to have a much lower market share and yet still exert enormous influence on the market. This is why the government defines a monopoly as being where a firm has 25% or more market share. Quite often a monopoly is able to restrict competition, reduce output and raise price in order to gain high excess profits. (Note: 'excess profits' refers to those profits in excess of the amount required to keep a firm in the industry — it is similar to the everyday use of the term 'profit' where revenue exceeds costs.) A number of markets in the UK show evidence of monopoly power, for example, Coca-Cola in soft drinks, Interbrew in beer sales and Microsoft in computer operating systems.

A firm with monopoly power may conduct restrictive practices, which reduce competition by:
- forming agreements with rival firms to fix prices at a high level (also known as collusion). Oil producers have attempted to undertake price fixing.
- dictating prices at which retailers are to sell its goods (often used by motor vehicle manufacturers to their dealers)
- restricting access to raw materials (De Beers Corporation, controlling supplies of rough diamonds to cutters and polishers)
- creating barriers to entry by limit pricing (see p. 23)

The role of profits
One important function of profit is to act as a signal to firms to enter a market and increase production. This process creates more competition, greater consumer choice and lower prices. In the long run, as output rises and prices fall, the excess profits tend to be competed away. This is how competitive markets work.

However, in monopoly markets, barriers to entry exist which prevent new firms from coming into an industry. This means excess profits are made in the long run. The market fails because output should be higher and price lower, with more competing firms. Consumers are not in control of the market.

Types of entry barriers to a market

High start-up costs

In some markets the start-up costs are so large that it is impractical for new firms to enter. For example, to compete in banking, iron and steel or pharmaceuticals, a firm may have to invest tens of millions of pounds in buildings and equipment.

Economies of scale

In some markets, massive economies of scale occur which enable the incumbent firms to produce at low unit costs. These firms also tend to have large market shares, which make market entry very difficult. A new entrant would usually have a relatively low output and high unit cost, making it very difficult for it to compete. Examples include mobile telephones, motor vehicle tyres and oil production.

Due to the enormous benefits from economies of scale, many markets can only sustain a few large firms. In extreme cases, there may only be room for one large firm. This represents a **natural monopoly**, where one firm captures all the economies of scale available in a particular industry. Examples include regional water companies and the postal letter delivery service.

Limit pricing

A powerful firm could deliberately set price at a level which is below the unit cost of potential entrants to an industry. This would cause new entrants to make a loss and so discourage them from entering the market.

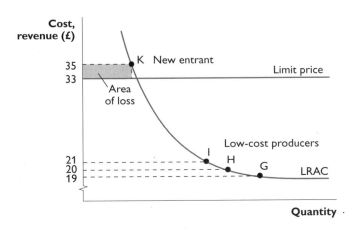

Figure 6 Limit pricing

Figure 6 shows the long-run average cost curve facing all firms in a particular industry. The established firms have already secured significant market share and economies of scale. They are shown at points G, H and I along the average cost curve; their average costs of production are £19, £20 and £21 respectively. However, a new entrant can only expect to secure a small market share and to build up its customer base slowly. Consequently, it is unable to gain the benefits from economies of scale and so faces higher average costs of production at £35 (position K on the cost curve).

The established firms estimate what the market share and average costs of a new entrant might be and then deliberately set price just below this level at £33. This price is sufficient to enable the established firms to make a healthy profit, while at the same time causing the new entrant to make a loss of £2 per unit of output. Potential entrants to the industry are scared off, realising that losses are likely to be made for a considerable time.

Control of market outlets

A firm may gain control of market outlets and prevent rival firms from using them. Examples include oil companies taking over petrol stations, breweries taking over pubs, and motorcycle companies controlling motorcycle dealers.

Control of market supplies

A firm may take control of vital raw materials or components in the production of a particular good. By cornering the commodity market for a good it can push up price and restrict sales to its competitors. The De Beers company is often cited as an example: it controls global 'rough' diamond sales through its Central Selling Organisation.

Advertising expenditure

Large firms tend to have large advertising budgets. The purpose of advertising is to increase sales and profits via the creation of brand loyalty. This should result in demand increasing and becoming more price inelastic over time. New entrants to an industry will need to budget for advertising in order to secure their own customers, but this could run into millions of pounds. The advertising budgets of soap powder manufacturers and chocolate confectioners run into millions of pounds every year.

Patents, copyright and licensing regulations

A firm may protect a new invention or innovation by obtaining a patent from the government Patents Office. A patent grants the owner a monopoly on the product for up to 20 years. In 2000, in the High Court, Dyson successfully stopped Hoover producing vacuum cleaners which had infringed the patent rights on cyclone suction technology.

Copyright laws protect the owners of films, music, books and articles from others copying them without the permission of the owners. In the UK the Copyright Licensing Agency monitors and enforces copyright laws.

The government can create barriers to entry through licensing regulations. For example, Virgin Rail has a licence to operate the west coast mainline railway service between London Euston and Glasgow Central; it effectively has a monopoly position on intercity services and faces limited competition from provincial rail operating firms.

A comparison of monopoly and competitive markets

Table 2 helps to explain why monopolies rather than competitive industries lead to market failure.

Table 2 Monopoly markets vs competitive markets

Monopoly market	Competitive market
Single producer: limited consumer choice.	Many producers: more consumer choice.
Output tends to be restricted due to absence of competition.	Output tends to be high due to fierce competition.
Price tends to be high due to absence of competition.	Price tends to be low due to fierce competition.
Firm tends to be a price-maker.	Firms tend to be price-takers.
Excess profits tend to be high and exist in the long run.	Excess profits tend to be competed away in the long run.
Entry and exit barriers to the industry exist.	Free entry and exit to the industry.
The absence of competition gives little incentive for a monopoly to improve product quality or provide a high degree of customer service.	The existence of competition gives an incentive for firms to improve product quality and provide a high degree of customer service.
Allocative and productive inefficiency due to lack of competition.	Allocative and productive efficiency in the perfect competition model.

Underprovision of public goods: missing markets

Some goods may not be produced at all through the price mechanism despite offering significant benefits to society. Where this occurs it is known as a **missing market** and the goods are called **public goods**. Public goods involve a large element of collective consumption and examples include national defence, flood defence schemes, the criminal justice system, refuse collection, firework displays, lighthouses and street lighting. Public goods are defined by two main characteristics:

(1) Non-rivalry in consumption. More people can consume the good without reducing the amount available for others, i.e. the good is non-diminishable. This means that the cost of supplying a public good to an extra consumer is zero.

(2) Non-exclusion in consumption. Once a public good has been provided, everyone is able to consume it, i.e. there are public property rights. People consume public goods whether they want to or not.

Private goods are the opposite of public goods. They display characteristics of rivalry and excludability in consumption. An example of a private good is the consumption of a chocolate bar, which directly excludes other people from consuming that particular one. The owners of private goods are able to exercise **private property rights**, preventing other people from consuming them. Private goods can be rejected, which means one has a choice over whether to consume them or not.

Problems of public goods
Free-rider problem

If left to free market forces, public goods would not be adequately provided for, despite the welfare gains a society can obtain from them. The market fails because firms cannot withhold the goods and services from people who refuse to pay and so there is a **free-rider problem**. Once the good has been provided for one individual, it is provided for all. Therefore, the rational consumer would wait for someone else to provide the good and then reap the benefits without paying for it. However, if everyone waits for others to provide the service then it may never be produced. The non-exclusive characteristic means a private market cannot develop since free riders do not pay.

Valuation problem

A second problem exists since it is difficult to measure the value obtained by the consumers of public goods and hence it becomes hard to establish a market price for them. It is in the interests of consumers to undervalue the utility gained in order to pay less for them, but it is in the interests of producers to overvalue the utility gained in order to charge more for them. This uncertainty over valuation may deter the provision of public goods.

Quasi-public goods

These possess some characteristics of public goods, for some but not all of the time. They are closer to pure public goods than private goods. Roads may be classed as quasi-public goods since the characteristic of non-rivalry over road space exists up to the point where congestion occurs. Once there is too much traffic, motorists become rivals for road space and roads cease to be public goods.

It may also be possible to exclude people from consuming quasi-public goods, for example, introducing tolls on motorways or electronic tags on vehicles during rush hour periods which will deter some users. This is an example of how a public good can be converted into a private good. Other examples of quasi-public goods include national health-care services, public parks and public beaches. Hospitals treat many patients every day but once they become full, waiting lists are created. Parks and beaches may also become full, preventing people from using them at certain times.

Government provision of public goods

In a mixed economy the government tends to provide public goods in order to correct market failure. It raises funds from general taxation to pay for their provision. Without government intervention, public goods would be underprovided or not provided at all. The actual quantity provided will be less than the quantity required for achieving the social optimum position (see p. 31).

Underprovision of merit goods: incomplete markets

A merit good is one which is underprovided by the price mechanism and it tends to yield more benefit to individuals than they realise. The value of these goods to the individual is not fully understood or appreciated and consequently insufficient resources are allocated to their production and consumption. Education, training and health-care services are often depicted as merit goods. If individuals were fully aware of the long-term benefits of these goods, more would be consumed.

The underconsumption of merit goods in a free market is shown in Figure 7, where the perceived benefit of consuming fresh fruit and vegetables on a regular basis is depicted by the demand curve D_2, leading to an equilibrium price of OP_2 and quantity OQ_2. However, the actual benefits to consumers are greater, indicated by demand curve D_3, where price should be at OP_3 and quantity OQ_3. The underprovision is shown by the distance between Q_2 and Q_3. (Remember that the demand curve represents the amount of benefit consumers gain from a good: higher demand means a higher level of benefit.)

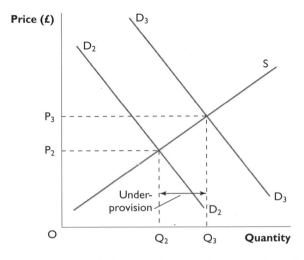

Figure 7 The market for fresh fruit and vegetables: examples of merit goods

Merit goods differ from positive externalities in that the former focus on the extra benefit to the individual concerned whilst the latter refer to benefits gained by others who are not part of the activity. However, **most merit goods yield positive externalities.** For example, students staying on at school in the sixth form are consuming a merit good since it is likely to increase their future earnings and offer wider career choices; it is also a positive externality since employers may gain from the increased productivity of more educated and skilled workers.

Merit goods can also be defined by the political process as 'those goods a government wants more to be consumed of in society'. Government intervention is often required to increase their provision and consumption, for example, the compulsory wearing of seat belts whilst travelling in a car or the use of crash helmets on motorbikes; even the legal requirement of firms to fit plugs to all electrical appliances before their sale to consumers in the UK is an example of government-inspired merit goods provision.

The underprovision of merit goods in society represents a market failure. The causes of this type of market failure can be traced back to several factors:

(1) The lack of information or knowledge of merit goods. People may not realise the full value of consuming merit goods such as using a health club regularly or obtaining vaccinations.

(2) The long-term nature of the benefits gained from merit goods. People tend to focus more on short-term rather than long-term benefits. For example, in the short run, under free market conditions, there is too little consumption of private insurance, dental care and education. However, later on in life many people regret this and wish they had consumed more.

(3) The unequal distribution of income and wealth. Some economists view inequality as a cause of market failure since many people may be unable to afford to buy merit goods, leading to underconsumption. For example, the low-paid, unemployed and sick may not have sufficient funds to afford private health-care insurance.

Overprovision of demerit goods

A demerit good is one which is overprovided by the price mechanism and tends to yield more cost to individuals than they realise. The dangers of such goods to the individual are not fully understood or recognised and consequently too many resources are allocated to their production, leading to overconsumption. Tobacco, alcohol and drugs are often depicted as demerit goods. If individuals were fully aware of the long-term harmful consequences of these goods, less would be consumed.

The overconsumption of demerit goods in a free market is shown in Figure 8, where the perceived benefit of consuming tobacco is depicted by the demand curve D_2, leading to an equilibrium price of OP_2 and quantity OQ_2. However, the actual net benefits to consumers are fewer, indicated by demand curve D_1, where price should be at OP_1 and quantity OQ_1. The term 'net benefit' refers to the benefit minus costs to individuals of consuming the good.

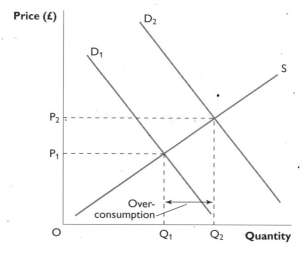

Figure 8 The market for tobacco

Demerit goods differ from negative externalities in that the former focus on the extra cost to the individual concerned whilst the latter refer to the costs imposed on others not part of the activity. However, **most demerit goods yield negative externalities**. Tobacco smokers are consuming a demerit good since it is likely to reduce their life expectancy, but it is also a negative externality since there will probably be increased absenteeism from work due to ill health and greater pressures placed upon the National Health Service.

Demerit goods can also be defined by the political process as 'those goods a government wants less to be consumed of in society'. Government intervention is often required to reduce their provision and consumption, for example, high taxation on tobacco and placing health warnings on cigarette packets.

The overprovision of demerit goods in society represents a market failure. As with merit goods, the causes can be traced back to imperfect market knowledge and the failure of consumers to value the long-term consequences of their decisions.

Externalities

An externality is **a cost or benefit which is external to an exchange**. It is a cause of market failure since the price mechanism fails to take account of such costs and benefits in the production and consumption of a good or service. Externalities are also known as **indirect costs and benefits**, **spillovers** or **third-party effects** since people who are not part of a transaction are affected.

External costs and benefits
- **An external cost in production** might be a chemical firm polluting a river with its waste. This causes an external cost to the fishing and water supply industries. Fish catches may be reduced and it may become very expensive to purify water to meet EU safety standards.
- **An external cost in consumption** of a good might be a person smoking tobacco in a pub or restaurant, polluting the air for other patrons. The effect is to cause passive smoking, where non-smokers may suffer from the same illnesses as smokers.
- **An external benefit in production** might be the recycling of waste materials such as newspaper, glass and tins. This has the benefit of reducing the amount of waste disposal for landfill sites. It also helps to promote sustainable economic growth.
- **An external benefit in consumption** of a good might be a person being vaccinated against various diseases. This reduces the possibility of other people catching a disease who come into contact with the vaccinated individual.

External costs are also known as **negative externalities** and external benefits as **positive externalities**. Further examples of external costs and benefits are shown in Table 3.

Table 3 Examples of external costs and benefits

	External costs	External benefits
Production	• Dumping of toxic waste at sea, which destroys fish life. • Overfishing, which depletes fish stocks. • Burning coal in power stations to create electricity, which adds to global warming.	• The location of a factory in an area of high unemployment, creating jobs directly and indirectly. • The construction of a new canal between Milton Keynes and Bedford, increasing tourism in the area.
Consumption	• Excess alcohol intake, which causes vandalism. • Adding to road traffic congestion when going on holiday.	• Education and training programmes, which increase human capital levels. • Improving the quality of one's garden, giving pleasure to neighbours. It could also increase property values.

In a free market, producers are only concerned with private costs of production — they ignore the external costs of production. The two types of costs added together are known as 'social costs'. **External costs represent the divergence between private costs and social costs**.

Private costs + External costs = Social costs

In a free market, consumers are only concerned with private benefits from consumption — they ignore the external benefits. The two types of benefits added together are known as 'social benefits'. **External benefits represent the divergence between private benefits and social benefits**.

Private benefits + External benefits = Social benefits

The market optimum output and price

In a free market, the equilibrium price and output occurs where the marginal private cost of production (MPC) is just equal to the marginal private benefit of consumption (MPB). This is the private equilibrium (or market equilibrium) output (see Figure 9).

The supply curve of the firm is its MPC curve. As a firm raises production in the short run it will face increasing marginal costs, and so to cover these extra costs it must be able to charge a higher price. This is why the supply curve slopes upwards from left to right.

The demand curve for consumers is the MPB curve. Economists assume it is possible to measure the benefit obtained from consuming a good by the price people are prepared to pay for it. As more of a good is consumed, the marginal utility or benefit will fall. This is why the demand curve slopes downwards from left to right. In Figure 9 the free market equilibrium price is OP_e and output OQ_e. It is the private optimum position, where MPC = MPB for the last unit produced.

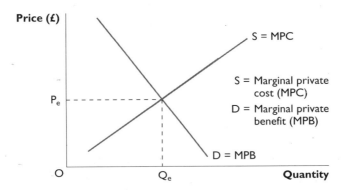

Figure 9 The free market optimum output and price

The social optimum output and price

The optimum provision of any good or service in society occurs when the marginal social benefit (MSB) obtained is equal to the marginal social cost (MSC) of producing it. This applies to public goods, private goods, merit and demerit goods. If provision is below the optimum, then MSC must be less than MSB. Welfare could be raised by increasing output. If provision is above the optimum, then MSB is less than MSC. Welfare could be raised by decreasing output. Figure 10 shows the social optimum price and output for society.

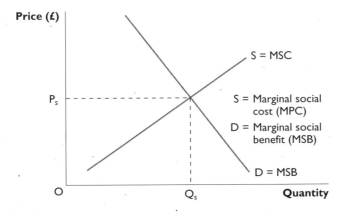

Figure 10 The social optimum price and output

External costs: production of a toxic chemical

The free market price mechanism ignores negative externalities. However, adding external costs onto the production of a good causes the supply curve of the firm to shift to the left and become the marginal social cost curve, shown in Figure 11. Assuming there are no external benefits in the production of the chemical good, the social optimum price is at OP_2 and output at OQ_2. When external costs are ignored there is underpricing and overproduction. There is an excess of social costs over social benefits for the marginal output between OQ_e and OQ_2.

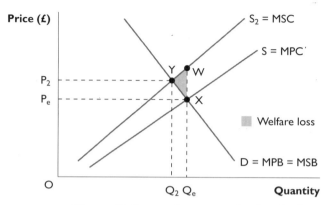

Figure 11 External costs: toxic chemicals

The marginal social cost of the slice of output Q_eQ_2 is Q_eWYQ_2 which exceeds the marginal social benefit of this output Q_eXYQ_2. The excess of costs over benefits is the shaded triangle XYW and this represents a welfare loss to society. The market has failed since negative externalities are ignored.

However, if the **external costs were internalised** into the market, output would fall to OQ_2 and price rise to OP_2. The welfare loss would be eliminated (see p. 41 on remedies for external costs).

In this example it is assumed that there are no external benefits and so marginal social benefit = marginal private benefit. The MSC curve is also sloping away from the MPC curve. This assumes external costs increase disproportionately with the increase in output. However, it is also possible to draw the MSC curve parallel to the MPC curve, indicating that the amount of external cost remains the same for each unit of output. Either drawing is valid.

External benefits: the consumption of a vaccination
The price mechanism in a free market ignores positive externalities. Adding external benefits to the consumption of a good causes the demand curve to shift to the right and become the marginal social benefit curve, shown in Figure 12. Assuming there are no external costs in the use of the vaccination, the social optimum price is OP_3 and output OQ_3. When external benefits are ignored there is underpricing and under-consumption of vaccinations in society.

The marginal social benefit of the slice of output Q_eQ_3 is Q_eMTQ_3 which exceeds the marginal social cost of this output Q_eZTQ_3. The excess of benefits over costs is the shaded triangle ZMT and this represents a potential welfare gain to society. However, the market has failed since positive externalities are ignored.

If external benefits were internalised into the market, output would rise to OQ_3 and price rise to OP_3. The welfare gain would be obtained. Nevertheless, it is unrealistic to assume that people will consume more and pay more for vaccinations. The market failure arises because consumers have imperfect market knowledge and are unaware of the full benefits of the vaccinations. The market failure could also arise because some consumers are unable to afford the vaccinations. This example shows how the types of market failure often overlap with each other.

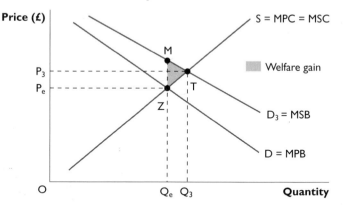

Figure 12 External benefits: vaccinations

Examination skills and concepts

- Defining market failure, government failure, monopoly, externalities, public goods, merit and demerit goods.
- Explaining the barriers to entry of new firms to a market.
- Understanding the distinction between private costs and social costs and illustrating this on a diagram.
- Understanding the distinction between private benefits and social benefits and illustrating this on a diagram.
- Drawing a diagram to distinguish between the private optimum and the social optimum price and output positions in a market.
- Illustrating the area of welfare loss on a diagram.
- Explaining the types of market failure in certain contexts. For example, road use, tobacco consumption, commercial fishing, production of chemicals, waste disposal, the burning of fossil fuels, the growth of tourism, health care and education provision.

Common examination errors

- Misinterpreting the instruction words within questions. For example, candidates may explain the case for and against an expansion of private health care when the question requires an *examination* of such a case.
- Incorrect drawing of diagrams showing external costs and external benefits.
- Inserting externality diagrams without any explanation or integration into the text.
- Drawing demand and supply graphs with the curves and axes labelled incorrectly.
- Numerical mistakes in calculating percentages and percentage change from economic data.

Links with other topics   There is a strong overlap between Units 1 and 2 in the AS specification. Market failure builds directly on the concepts and models of Unit 1, especially demand and supply analysis. It is common for exam questions in Unit 2 to

include determinants of demand and supply, which are equally at home in Unit 1; for example, causes of air traffic or road traffic growth in the UK. Further links include:
- Short-run and long-run costs (Unit 4).
- External costs and external benefits which build directly on demand and supply analysis (Unit 1).
- Productive and allocative efficiency (Unit 4).
- Monopoly and competitive markets (Unit 4).
- Types of barriers to entry (Unit 4).
- Economies of scale (Unit 4).
- Equity issues of health care and education (Unit 5A).

Remedies for market failure

There are several methods for correcting market failure, all of which involve government intervention. The purpose of government intervention is to overcome market failures. It can be classified broadly into regulation, direct controls and prohibition, tradable pollution permits, the extension of property rights, environmental taxation and subsidies. The type of remedy depends on the nature of the market failure.

Remedies for monopoly

The government uses two broad approaches in attempting to control monopoly power in the UK, i.e. regulation and the encouragement of entry of new firms to an industry.

(1) Regulation
This involves setting up rules for firms and then creating regulatory bodies to monitor and enforce them. Usually the regulations are backed up by government legislation.
- **The Office of Fair Trading** has powers to investigate markets and decide whether firms are acting in the public interest. It provides the government with advice on monopolies, mergers and restrictive practices.
- **The Competition Commission** can investigate proposed mergers between firms and recommend whether they should proceed. If a merger leads to a market share of 25% or more, it is likely that the Competition Commission will block it. For example, Interbrew (the Belgian brewery) purchased Bass brewery whilst owning Whitbread. It currently has 40% of the UK beer market and consequently it has to sell one of its two UK breweries. The Competition Commission also has powers to investigate firms which may be abusing their monopoly power and so acting against the public interest.
- **The regulatory bodies** set up in the utility industries can 'price cap' firms. This involves restricting the price rise of a utility to the formula: 'RPI – X%'. RPI refers to the retail price index and represents the rate of inflation for a given year; X% is a figure determined by the regulator and is based on predicted efficiency gains in

the industry. The regulator wants some of these gains to be passed on to consumers in the form of lower real prices.

The regulatory bodies can also establish service agreements with utility firms. For example, in the rail industry, targets are set for train operators for punctuality, cancellations and the number of services per route per day. The regulatory bodies include: OFGEM (Office for Gas and Electricity Market); OFTEL (Office for Telecommunication Services); OFWAT (Office for Water Services); Postcomm (Postal Services Commission); and SRA (Strategic Rail Authority).

- **The regulation of restrictive trade practices** between firms is controlled by the **Restrictive Practices Court**, which investigates business agreements and can declare them illegal. Firms are legally required to register any trade agreements that restrict competition, for example, price agreements or the sharing of company patents.

(2) Promotion of market entry

The government also promotes the entry of new firms and their growth in markets to enhance competition. Some of the measures it uses to do this are listed below:

- **Deregulation**, e.g. the letter delivery service. The Post Office has been converted into a public limited company (formerly called Consignia but now known as the Royal Mail) where the government is the single shareholder. A regulator called Postcomm has also been set up in the industry. The regulator has invited other firms to enter the bulk mail delivery service to compete against the Royal Mail, with entry to the market expected by 2006.
- **Training and Enterprise Councils (TECs).** The government set up 82 TECs in England and Wales for the purpose of promoting enterprise in local areas. This includes offering free courses on how to set up and run a business. The impact has been to assist in the creation of small firms in many different markets.
- **Loan Guarantee Scheme.** This enables small businesses with insufficient collateral to borrow from a commercial bank, the repayment being guaranteed by the government if the firm were to default. Up to £100,000 can be borrowed for a maximum period of 10 years. The scheme is only available for small businesses which have been unable to obtain a loan yet have a viable business proposition. It enables the firms to get established and grow more easily.
- **Favourable corporation tax rates.** In the April 2002 budget, the government reduced the rate of corporation tax on profits for small firms from 20% to 19%. Furthermore, the lower corporation tax rate for small firms with profits less than £10,000 was changed from 10% to zero. These tax changes should help the growth of small firms which may offer more competition against the larger firms.

Remedies for external costs and demerit goods

There are several forms of government intervention which include **direct controls, tradable permits, the extension of property rights, taxation** and **subsidies**. The purpose is to reduce the production and consumption of both external costs and demerit goods.

(1) Direct controls
Restriction

To reduce the external costs from economic activities that create a significant amount of pollution, the government has set restrictions for many factories in the UK. The Environmental Protection Act (1989) set minimum environmental standards for emissions from over 3,500 factories involved in chemical processes, waste incineration and oil refining. Firms are monitored by Her Majesty's Inspectorate of Pollution and in extreme cases the inspectors can close down a factory.

Advantages of pollution restrictions
- clear pollution limits set
- possible to close down major polluters

Disadvantages of pollution restrictions
- expensive to monitor firms
- extra administration costs for firms
- difficult to quantify and attach a monetary value to the pollution
- direct controls operate against the market, overruling it completely rather than working with it
- direct controls could even lead to government failure if the regulations serve to misallocate resources

Prohibition

One form of direct control is to prohibit the production of certain high polluting goods. If the pollution cost from each unit of a good exceeds the benefit gained from it, the government should impose a ban on production. This is shown in Figure 13, where the marginal pollution cost (MPC) exceeds net marginal private benefit (NMPB) at all levels of output.

The marginal cost of pollution curve (MPC) shows the amount of pollution generated from one extra unit of output. The curve gets steeper as output increases since it becomes harder for the environment to cope with larger quantities of pollution and so more damage is done.

The net marginal private benefit curve (NMPB) is the excess of private benefit over the private cost of producing one extra unit of a good for the firm. (Note that in this case private benefits refer to the revenue obtained by the firm and not the consumer.) The NMPB curve represents the profit obtained by producing one further unit of a good. In effect, it is a firm's revenue minus its cost of each additional unit of output. The NMPB curve falls as output increases since marginal costs of production tend to rise rapidly due to diminishing returns setting in.

It is rational for a government to ban the production of goods which yield higher pollution costs to society than private benefits to firms, for example, highly toxic chemical compounds.

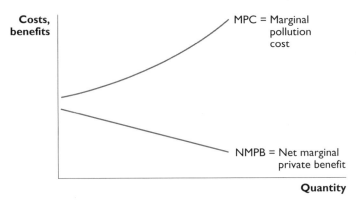

Figure 13 Prohibition on the production of a good

Restriction and prohibition of demerit goods

To reduce the consumption of demerit goods such as alcohol and tobacco, the government has passed legislation which prohibits sales to children. Restrictions are also applied according to the time and place of sale, for example, limited opening hours for pubs and off-licences. There are also restrictions on the advertising of alcohol and tobacco. Indeed, the UK government is considering a ban on all tobacco advertising. Unfortunately, teenage consumption of alcohol and tobacco is quite widespread, suggesting that the law is an ineffective method of control.

The case of illegal drugs: a demerit good

Illegal drugs such as heroin and cocaine are demerit goods which often have high levels of external costs associated with their use. As consumers become addicted to these drugs they may have difficulty in financing their 'fixes' and so turn to crimes such as burglary and prostitution. There is also an incentive for drug-users to become suppliers in order to pay for their addictive needs.

Government intervention to correct market failure focuses on reducing both supply and demand. On the supply side, the government created the post of an anti-drugs coordinator with far reaching powers to wage war against drug-pushers. Police forces around the country have special units to deal with drug-related crimes and the Customs and Excise department allocates many of its resources to catching drug smugglers. Convicted drug suppliers are also likely to face stiff prison sentences. The effect of decreasing supply is shown in Figure 14. A successful drug enforcement policy shifts the supply curve from S to S_1 (leaving demand at D).

The more successful the authorities are in reducing the supply of illegal drugs on the open market, the higher the price of these drugs will tend to rise, as shown in Figure 14. The price of drugs increases from OP_e to OP_1. Unfortunately, the high price then encourages more people to enter the market for supplying drugs, since the potential profits are considerable.

On the demand side, government policies include various measures to discourage drug consumption. These may be in the form of education programmes in schools and colleges, shock advertising campaigns, random drug-testing to deter users and tougher sentences for trafficking and possession. Policies have also focused on treating drug addiction as a medical problem; patients are given a legal supply of a substitute drug whilst rehabilitation measures are made available. The effect of these measures is to shift the demand curve from D to D_1 as shown in Figure 14.

If the combination of these policies is effective in reducing the consumption of illegal drugs, the market price and quantity should fall to OP_0 and OQ_0 respectively.

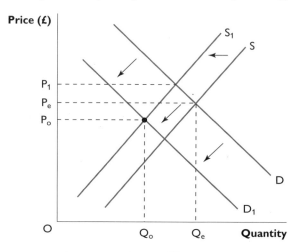

Figure 14 The market for illegal drugs

(2) Tradable permits

Tradable permits (marketable permits) involve the government setting a quantitative limit (quota) on the amount of pollution allowed in an industry and then allocating pollution permits to individual firms. Each firm is allowed to pollute up to the level set by its permit. It is also possible for firms to buy and sell any surplus permits, or to bank them for use in future years.

The American electricity generation industry

Tradable permits are used in the American electricity generation industry to reduce the effects of acid rain. This type of pollution is caused by sulphur dioxide and nitrogen oxide emissions from power stations. It leads to the acidification of lakes and streams, killing fish as well as damaging soils, trees and buildings.

Since 1995, the American Environmental Protection Agency (EPA) has set limits on sulphur and nitrogen oxide emissions. The electricity generating plants were required to install standard equipment to monitor these emissions. Each power station was then allocated a pollution allowance based on its previous consumption rates. The sulphur dioxide allowances were split into 1 ton units, totalling 8.95 million tons for the whole industry per year. The cleaner electricity generation firms were able to pollute below their maximum limits and sell excess allowances to other firms who had older, dirtier plants. One ton of sulphur dioxide pollution allowance is priced at around $1,500. The pollution permits cover more than 2,000 coal, oil and gas burning plants in the USA and have been effective in reducing sulphur dioxide emissions by 40%.

The optimum pollution permit

Tradable permits give rise to the question of what should be the total quantity of pollution allowed for an industry. This is answered by Figure 15. The firm would maximise its profits when output is at Q250 units, where the net marginal private benefit (NMPB) is equal to zero (the last unit of output yields no addition to total profits, unlike each of the previous units). However, at output Q250 there are significant pollution costs which are ignored under a free market.

The optimum position for society would be at output Q200 units, where pollution costs are taken into account. At the 200th unit of output, the marginal pollution cost of $15 is equated with the net marginal private benefit to the firm, also $15. The government could intervene by issuing pollution permits to firms, at a cost of $15 per unit of output. This would cause firms to cut production to Q200 units per period.

The optimum amount of pollution would be that generated by 200 units of output, with a permit price of $15 per unit of output. The revenue obtained by the government in charging firms for pollution permits could then be allocated to the sufferers.

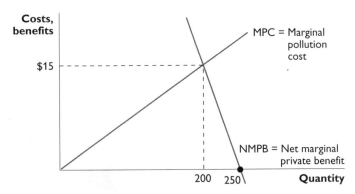

Figure 15 The optimum pollution permit:
electricity generation from a power station

Advantages of issuing pollution permits
- Pollution allowances can be reduced over time as part of a coordinated plan by the government.
- The government can charge firms for the right to pollute which helps to internalise the negative externality.
- By charging for pollution permits the government collects funds for cleaning up the environmental damage created or for compensating sufferers.
- It increases production costs for major polluters whilst assisting cleaner firms which are able to sell their excess pollution allowances.
- Firms have an incentive to invest in clean technology.

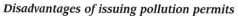

Disadvantages of issuing pollution permits

- They increase production costs for firms, which could reduce their international competitiveness if the pollution permits are not applied by other governments overseas.
- There is less pressure on major polluting firms to clean up their acts if it is possible to buy extra permits from elsewhere.
- The valuation of pollution costs is an inexact science and varies between groups within society and also between generations. For example, Friends of the Earth may place a higher value on environmental damage caused by gravel extraction than the construction firms that are set to gain profits from the activity. Similarly, future generations may place a much higher value on the pollution created from today's nuclear power plants than the current generation does.
- The cost to the government of monitoring pollution is likely to be high.

(3) Extending property rights

This involves the government allocating ownership rights to organisations over the use of certain resources, for example, the air, rivers and seas. All too often, negative externalities arise due to the absence of property rights. Indeed, there is an incentive to abuse the resources if no property rights exist. Consequently, the government has allocated property rights in certain circumstances.

In 1989, the government set up the National Rivers Authority and gave it property rights to rivers, streams, lakes and coastal waters in England and Wales. This organisation is responsible for safeguarding and improving the natural water environment. It restricts pollution levels and can prosecute firms for illegal spillage, making them pay for the damage caused.

The government has also extended property rights to workers, which enable them to sue their employers for compensation if gross negligence is suspected. For example, asbestos workers who suffer from the deadly disease asbestosis have taken their former employers to court, seeking damages. The outcome has led to a large reduction in the production of asbestos worldwide.

Advantages

- There is an increase in knowledge and expertise for the organisation with the property right. It takes the pressure away from the government to assess the pollution.
- There is a greater likelihood that resources will be managed carefully to ensure their availability for future generations.
- The property owners can charge firms which need to pollute the environment. The funds can be used to clean up the environment or compensate sufferers.
- Firms which damage the environment without permission can be prosecuted and made to pay for clean-up operations.

Disadvantages

- It is often difficult for a government to extend property rights. For example, UK membership of the European Union means EU fishing boats are entitled to fish in

UK territorial waters. Imposing restrictions on fishing would have to apply not just to UK fishing boats but to all EU fishing vessels.
- It could be difficult to trace the source of the environmental damage. In the case of asbestosis sufferers who worked for more than one asbestos company, it has been extremely difficult to prove which firm caused the disease. Consequently, compensation payments have been withheld.
- The legal costs involved in prosecuting a polluter could be extremely high, deterring victims from taking action.
- There is likely to be an imperfect transfer of funds from polluters to sufferers.
- The compensation process from polluter to victim could take years to resolve. In some cases the sufferer dies during legal proceedings.

(4) Environmental taxes

The government could impose a tax on the polluting firms in order to internalise the externality. In order to do this it would need to make an accurate assessment of the cost of the pollution and then impose a tax equal to the value of the pollution.

Figure 16 shows the market for petrol, including both the marginal private cost curve (MPC) and the marginal social cost curve (MSC). In a free market the equilibrium price is OP_e and quantity OQ_e. However, the social optimum price is OP_1 and quantity OQ_1, where marginal social costs equal marginal social benefits (MSB) of the last unit produced. The vertical distance ZY represents the external cost (air pollution) for each litre of petrol consumed.

By placing a tax equal to the external cost of ZY per litre, the government success-fully internalises the pollution. The total tax collected is shown by the area P_1YZP_o. Both producers and consumers pay the tax, depending upon the relative elasticities of demand and supply. The consumer tax area is YP_1P_eT and the producer tax is P_eP_oZT.

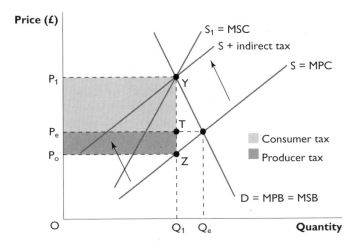

Figure 16 The imposition of a specific tax on petrol

Advantages

- Environmental taxes are based on the principle that the polluter pays — in the above example this means both the producers and consumers.
- The heaviest polluters pay more tax whilst those who pollute least pay less tax and have greater opportunities for expanding their businesses.
- Environmental taxes work with market forces, helping to internalise the externality whilst maintaining consumer choice.
- Tax funds are raised for the government and these could be used to clean up the environment or to compensate sufferers.

Disadvantages

- It is difficult to measure the amount of pollution and then place a monetary value on it.
- In the above example transport costs are increased, which could lead to higher production costs for firms and higher general inflation.
- Firms may relocate to other countries with less stringent environmental taxes.
- The demand for petrol, for example, tends to be price inelastic and so the overall reduction in pollution levels may be small.

Road pricing

Road pricing can be regarded as a form of taxation for road use. There are two main types of road pricing. The first is the use of tolls as seen on motorways in France: motorists pay a fee at tollbooths located at various strategic points along a major road. The second type involves electronic tagging of motor vehicles: each vehicle is fitted with a meter and a smart card that is tracked by satellites; the satellite records where a vehicle goes and sends a bill to the owner according to the type of road and the time used. Electronic metering of motor vehicles has been in operation for several years on roads in Singapore.

Advantages

- It internalises the externality, creating a more efficient resource allocation. The metering of vehicles is a flexible system, which can be used to equate the marginal social cost with the marginal social benefit of the last journey conducted.
- It raises tax revenue, which can be used to improve public transport or pay for road construction schemes.
- Alternatively, it might enable the government to reduce other forms of taxation on motorists, such as road and fuel duties. This option is supported by Professor David Begg, economist and chairman of the Commission for Integrated Transport. He suggested the annual road tax of £160 could be scrapped and that fuel tax could fall by 10p per litre.
- It could be regarded as fair since motorists involved in traffic jams are billed for them directly. Indeed, road pricing might be fairer than the road tax licence and petrol duties, which are indiscriminate since they apply to all motorists irrespective of whether congestion is caused.

- It could also:
  - reduce traffic congestion as motorists find alternative routes or alternative times to use major roads
  - reduce non-essential journeys
  - reduce the consumption of a non-renewable resource and the pollution associated with it
  - reduce the number of accidents on tolled roads
  - increase the flow of traffic, possibly reducing overall transport costs for road haulage firms
  - encourage more people to work locally or at home

Disadvantages

- It could be regarded as unfair since road pricing is a regressive tax. Low income earners with motor vehicles could pay a higher percentage of their income in road tolls.
- It could increase transport costs for road haulage firms and thus lead to higher prices for goods and services. Labour costs to firms could also increase if they decided to compensate staff by paying the road tolls for them.
- It could encourage motorists to find alternative routes, which are unsuitable for heavy traffic, e.g. country lanes and villages. This could lead to considerable damage to minor roads.
- Electronic tagging is a very expensive system to set up and the cost is likely to be passed on to motorists.
- It could reduce the size of the labour market for individual firms as workers seek employment closer to their homes in order to avoid road tolls.
- If more people work from home it could reduce overall labour productivity.
- Industries which supply complementary goods to road users could face a decrease in demand, e.g. motor vehicles and petroleum.
- There could be a loss of trade for firms along tolled routes, e.g. shops, petrol stations and restaurants.
- Public transport is in a very poor state. Bus and train companies are unlikely to cope with the extra passenger demand that would arise if motorists left their cars at home.

(5) Subsidies of cleaner alternatives

A subsidy is a grant provided by the government to encourage the production and consumption of a particular good or service. In order to reduce external costs, the government could subsidise cleaner alternatives. For example, gas is a cleaner fuel than coal or oil, so the government has subsidised the construction of gas-fired power stations. This has led to a reduction in carbon dioxide emissions and assisted the UK government in achieving its Kyoto targets of cutting emissions of greenhouse gases along with 38 other industrial nations by an overall rate of 5.2% by 2008–12.

Many governments around the world subsidise public transport systems in order to reduce the number of private vehicles on the road, leading to less congestion, air and noise pollution. Figure 17(a) shows the application of a unit subsidy to a market for bus travel. The effect of a subsidy is to lower the price of each bus journey from OP_e to OP_1 and increase the quantity of users from OQ_e to OQ_1. The subsidy is deducted vertically from the original market supply curve S, effectively shifting it to S_1.

The subsidy per unit is AB and the total subsidy area is $ABCP_1$. Part of the subsidy is passed on to consumers in the form of a lower price for bus travel, equal to the area AGP_eP_1. The other portion of the subsidy ($GBCP_e$) remains with the producer.

The lower price of bus travel should cause a decrease in demand for private motor use, shown by the shift of the demand curve to D_1 in Figure 17(b).

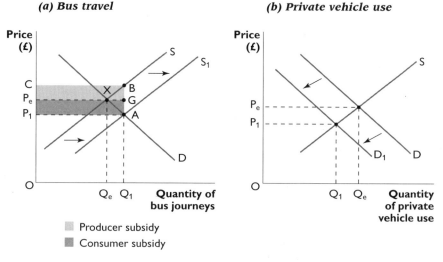

(a) Bus travel

(b) Private vehicle use

Producer subsidy
Consumer subsidy

*Figure 17 A unit subsidy for bus travel and
the impact on the market for private vehicle use*

Advantages of public transport subsidies

- Public transport subsidies should lead to a reduction in road traffic congestion and vehicle journey times, possibly reducing transport costs for firms.
- Less atmospheric and noise pollution.
- More efficient use of scarce resources such as petrol and road space.
- An increase in consumer surplus of area XAP_1P_e shown in Figure 17(a).

Disadvantages of public transport subsidies

- Subsidies are expensive for the government to fund (shown by area $ABCP_1$ in Figure 17(a).
- Bus and rail operators may become inefficient in production if they rely on subsidies.
- Public transport tends to be an inferior good and so a reduction in price might have little effect on increasing the number of passengers.

Remedies for public goods, merit goods and external benefits

Public goods

There is little room to manoeuvre around the free-rider problem experienced in the market for pure public goods. Consequently, it is common practice for the government to fund their provision and then collect the monies from general taxation. In the financial year 2002–03, the government plans to spend £24 billion on defence and a further £23 billion on law and order out of a total public expenditure of £420 billion. This represents 11.2% of all government spending. In order to pay for these public goods, taxes are levied on incomes and expenditure. Both defence and law and order can be regarded as public goods.

In the case of quasi-public goods there may be scope to introduce private charging, as in the case of road pricing and entry to parks.

Merit goods

The government also tends to fund merit goods from general taxation, for example, education, training and health care, though these activities have strong private sector provision too. Figure 18 shows the application of a government subsidy to higher education institutions in order to increase the number of students.

Before the subsidy is applied, the market equilibrium price is £5,000 per year and 500,000 university places are taken up. The market optimum is reached where marginal private costs equal marginal private benefits for the last student. (It is assumed there are no external costs and so MPC = MSC.)

However, to reach the social optimum quantity, the government subsidises student fees, which has the effect of shifting the supply curve to S_2. This increases student numbers to 800,000 and reduces fees to £1,100 per person per year. The marginal social benefit equals the marginal social cost of the last university place taken up.

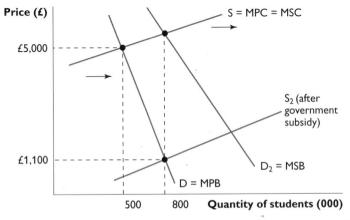

Figure 18 The application of a subsidy to higher education

Advantages of subsidising higher education

- Subsidies are likely to increase the number of students in higher education and raise human capital levels of the workforce. This should lead to greater productivity and international competitiveness of the UK economy.
- An increase in the number of graduates should help reduce the skills shortage and raise the pool of labour for firms to choose from.
- Subsidies help reduce inequality within society as more people from low-income backgrounds are able to take higher education courses.
- Graduates are likely to have higher salaries than non-graduates. The Career Services Unit has recently published a report indicating that graduates earn around £15,000 more per year than non-graduates by the time they reach middle-age.
- External benefits are internalised, moving towards the social optimum allocation of resources.

Disadvantages of subsidising higher education

- Subsidising higher education is very expensive for the government and entails an opportunity cost. For example, the funds could have been spent on reducing hospital waiting lists or improving public transport.
- The government may have to increase taxation to continue funding higher education.
- A significant proportion of higher education students drop out of their courses, representing a waste of government funds. If students had to pay the full cost of their studies, the dropout rate would probably be lower.
- Graduates in some subjects tend to suffer from high levels of unemployment, for example, the arts and humanities. This suggests an excess supply of graduates in some labour markets and a misallocation of resources.

Examination skills and concepts
- Outlining government measures for regulating monopolies and promoting competition.
- Explaining the advantages and disadvantages of tradable permits to control pollution.
- Explaining the advantages and disadvantages of extending property rights to reduce pollution of rivers and seas.
- Explaining how subsidiaries may increase the provision of merit goods.
- Recognising the important role of government in the provision of public goods.
- Explaining how indirect taxes may decrease the provision of demerit goods.

Common examination errors
- Misinterpreting the instruction words within questions. For example, candidates may simply list arguments for and against road pricing schemes, when the question requires an evaluation of such schemes.
- Incorrect drawing of a diagram to show how indirect taxes may internalise external costs.
- Incorrect drawing of a diagram to show how subsidiaries may internalise external benefits.

Links with other topics
- Government regulation of monopolies (Unit 4).

- Government measures to promote the growth of new firms (Unit 4).
- Application of indirect taxes and subsidiaries (Unit 1).
- The significance of elasticity in determining the effects of indirect taxes and subsidiaries for correcting market failure (Unit 1).

Government failure

Government failure occurs when government intervention in markets leads to economic inefficiency, and therefore a net loss in economic welfare. There are several causes including a lack of market information, the distortion of market forces, conflicts in government objectives, regulatory capture and time lags as outlined below.

Lack of market information

The government intervenes to correct market failure in various ways, but a lack of information may cause it to make inappropriate decisions. The following examples show how this occurs.

Setting the tax level to internalise external costs

The government imposes both excise tax and value added tax (VAT) on goods which yield negative externalities, for example, tobacco and alcohol. However, a move to the social optimum position in the market requires precise information on the amount of external cost for each unit of output. This is very difficult to acquire. The cost to an individual who gets cancer from passive smoking is incalculable to that person. If the government sets too low a tax on a demerit good, there is likely to be over-production and underpricing.

Setting a subsidy to increase consumption of merit goods

The government may subsidise merit goods in order to increase consumption of them, for example subsidising higher education courses. However, a move to the social optimum position requires precise information on the amount of external benefit for each unit of service consumed. Again, this is very difficult to acquire. The additional benefit to people who take university courses varies from one person to another. If the government provides too low a subsidy per course, there is likely to be under-provision and overpricing.

Provision of public goods

The government needs to fund public goods provision, such as defence and law and order. However, how much to spend on these areas depends to a large extent on politics rather than economics. Traditionally, Conservative governments have spent more on these types of goods than Labour governments, believing defence of the realm and domestic security is of paramount importance. The decisions made depend more on value judgements than facts.

High levels of government spending on public goods mean more taxes or less government spending elsewhere, such as on the provision of merit goods. Low levels of government spending on public goods mean lower taxes or more funding of merit goods. The public elects the government which makes these decisions, but a general election occurs only once every 4–5 years. Furthermore, public voting for a political party often involves many other factors besides public goods provision (for example, policy towards asylum seekers, the single European currency and transport). Consequently, the public may have insufficient information to make accurate decisions on which political party to vote for.

Distortion of market forces

Government intervention to correct market failure may actually lead to more serious problems overall, particularly in agricultural, housing and labour markets.

A guaranteed minimum price for agricultural commodities

The government may intervene to stabilise agricultural prices and boost farm incomes. However, by setting a minimum guaranteed price for agricultural goods which is far above the free market price, large surpluses will be created. To maintain the scheme, these have to be purchased and stored by the government, representing a substantial cost to taxpayers.

This is shown in Figure 19, where a minimum price of OP_2 leads to an excess supply of Q_1Q_2 in wheat production. Government expenditure on the surplus is depicted by the area Q_1Q_2YX.

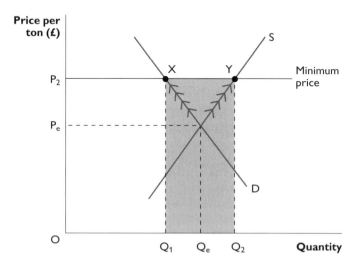

Figure 19 The effects of a guaranteed minimum price on the wheat market

There is also the problem of how to dispose of the food surpluses. Over time they will rot, but dumping them in overseas markets could disrupt the agricultural systems in other countries and invite criticism from the World Trade Organisation or even retaliation from other countries. Destroying the surpluses represents a complete waste of resources.

The European Commission has operated a minimum pricing policy for more than 40 years in agricultural markets, known as the Common Agricultural Policy (CAP). Almost half the European Commission's budget is spent on the CAP. This represents a misallocation of resources since the agricultural markets fail to reach equilibrium position. There is allocative inefficiency.

Over recent years, the European Commission has reduced funding of the CAP, preferring to pay farmers for managing the countryside rather than producing food surpluses. This trend is likely to continue but will meet fierce resistance from many farmers throughout the European Union.

The national minimum wage

The government appears to face a trade-off in determining the level of the national minimum wage. If the minimum wage is set at too high a level, then it will reduce poverty among the low paid who keep their jobs, but at the cost of some of them becoming unemployed. This is shown by a minimum wage of OW_2 in Figure 20, which causes a significant fall in employment by the amount $Q_e - Q_1$. If the national minimum wage is set at too low a level, then it will have little impact on reducing poverty among low-paid workers. This is shown by a minimum wage of OW_1 which has no effect on the labour market.

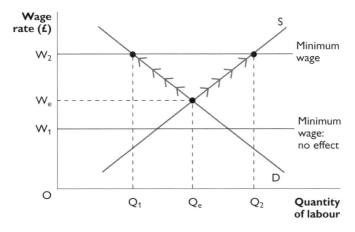

Figure 20 *The effects of setting different minimum wage rates*

Income tax levels

The largest source of revenue for the government comes from income taxation. There are two main tax rates: the basic rate of 22% and the top rate of 40%. These are marginal tax rates, so people only pay these tax rates once their income rises to a certain level.

The main problem is that if income tax is set at too high a level, then it reduces the incentive to work and also encourages tax evasion. High income taxes could cause a fall in output and employment levels, eventually worsening government finances. The economy may become less competitive.

Expenditure tax levels

The government imposes both VAT and excise taxes on certain goods and services. This may be desirable for demerit goods, but many other goods and services are affected too. Expenditure taxes lead to a fall in consumer and producer surplus, creating a dead weight loss, shown in Figure 21.

A specific tax has the effect of shifting supply from S to S_1. The vertical distance between the two supply curves is the tax per unit of output. The equilibrium price rises from OP_e to OP_1. The tax area is XP_1PC. The loss of consumer surplus is P_1P_eZX, of which ZXB is dead weight loss. The loss of producer surplus is $ZCPP_e$, of which ZCB is dead weight loss.

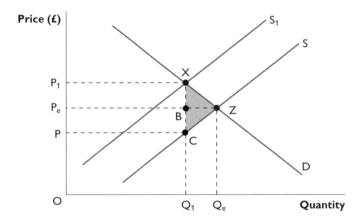

Figure 21 Dead weight loss from an expenditure tax

Benefit and tax credit levels

The government has a system of benefits and tax credits to redistribute income in society. Benefits include the Job Seekers' Allowance to help people who are unemployed. If the benefit level is set too high it may discourage people from genuinely seeking work, but if the benefit level is set too low it does little to alleviate poverty. The government needs to get the right balance between offering financial assistance to overcome hardship and maintaining the incentive to work.

The Chancellor of the Exchequer, Gordon Brown, will be remembered for the introduction of various tax credit schemes, aimed at reducing poverty and increasing work incentives. They include the Working Family Tax Credit which 'tops up' the pay of a working household with a disposable income below a certain level. The government payment is made through employers who increase the take-home pay of the family income earner and then offset this from their own tax returns. The effect is to boost the pay of low-income households and increase incentives to work.

However, some critics claim that tax credits are unnecessary if the income earner is already in work. Furthermore, tax credit schemes are expensive and complicated to administer, making additional costs for employers.

Maximum rent controls in the private rented housing market

The government may intervene in the private rented housing market to reduce exploitation of tenants by landlords. The government may set a maximum rent, which it perceives to be fair to both tenants and landlords. However, a rent control set below the market equilibrium price will cause a contraction in supply and expansion in demand, leading to a shortage of private rented property. Government intervention may have unwittingly created a housing shortage. This is shown in Figure 22, where the maximum rent is set at OR_1, below the equilibrium rent of OR_e, causing an excess demand over supply of accommodation of $Q_2 - Q_1$.

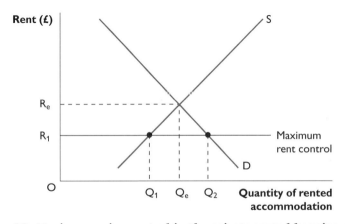

Figure 22   Maximum price control in the private rented housing market

Conflicts in government objectives

Economic efficiency vs equity

A government may face a tough choice in some markets over whether to improve economic efficiency or equity. Government intervention in markets is sometimes aimed at redistributing income and wealth, creating a fairer society (the equity case). However, this may reduce economic efficiency directly. The following example shows how economic efficiency may be compromised in order to create a fairer society.

The fuel tax escalator

In 1993 the Conservative government introduced significant increases in taxes on petrol and other motor vehicle fuels, leading to an annual rise of 6% above the rate of inflation. This was known as the 'fuel tax escalator'. On coming to power in 1997, the Labour government intended to continue the hike in fuel taxes. This was justified on the grounds of economic efficiency, since the pollution generated causes over-consumption and underpricing in the market. Moreover, the fuel tax escalator could be seen as an environmental tax.

However, the higher fuel taxes could not be justified on equity grounds since they affected low-income earners more than high-income groups, forcing them off the roads. Petrol taxes are regressive. By September 1999, public unrest with the fuel taxes led to a series of protests at petrol stations and oil refineries around the UK. A 'dump the pump' campaign was set up and oil refineries were blockaded by disgruntled lorry drivers, leading to a petrol shortage and long queues outside petrol stations. The government was eventually forced to abandon the fuel tax escalator, sacrificing efficiency for equity.

Economic efficiency vs the environment

Economic efficiency could also clash with management of the environment, as revealed by the scaling back of government road-building programmes.

Scrapping plans to widen the M1 motorway

In the early 1990s, the government decided to abandon plans to widen the M1 motorway on the grounds of financial cost and environmental damage. This was popular with environmental campaigners but critics claim it has led to greater road traffic congestion and less investment along the motorway route, damaging business interests. In 2002 the government re-examined the possibility of widening the M1 in Bedfordshire and Buckinghamshire (junctions 10–14) but, again, decided against it.

The proposed household waste tax

Some government schemes sound fine in theory but are unworkable in practice, e.g. the proposed 'rubbish tax' to tackle Britain's mountain of household waste. This involves charging households an extra fee if they have more than two sacks of rubbish collected each week. However, low-income and large families would suffer disproportionately. Furthermore, households already pay for rubbish collection via council tax and so the extra charge would represent 'double-taxation'.

Several other problems would also arise from the 'rubbish tax'. It is likely to cause an increase in fly tipping or disputes between households over ownership of rubbish bags, especially in multiple-occupancy properties. It could also encourage people to put their rubbish into larger bags or take it to the council dumps themselves; they could even burn it in their gardens, creating atmospheric pollution.

Productive efficiency in rubbish collection is likely to decrease if refuse workers have to determine ownership of each bag collected as this would slow down the speed of the operation.

Regulatory capture

The government is responsible for regulating monopolies and it has created regulatory bodies for this purpose, particularly in the utility industries, e.g. gas, electricity, water, telecommunications and postal services. The regulator may price cap a utility through the formula RPI − X%, where the RPI represents inflation and '−X' represents the predicted efficiency gains to be passed on to consumers in the form of lower prices.

However, problems arise if the regulator operates in the interests of the utility rather than the consumers. This is known as 'regulatory capture' and it may arise through the close cooperation between the firm and regulator. The firm might be selective in the information given to the regulator; alternatively, it could bombard the regulator with masses of technical information, which is hard to decipher.

The utility might exaggerate its costs and underestimate revenues deliberately, in order to gain favourable treatment. As forecast profits are lower than they should be, the regulator will set a smaller –X figure. This enables more profits to be gained for the benefit of shareholders and company directors.

The –X figure is normally set every 4 to 5 years to allow stability in the industry before it is changed. Thus, large company profits can be made for several years and government intervention effectively fails to prevent customers paying too much for the services offered. Some economists believe that the water and electricity industries were more favourably treated than telecommunications and gas during the 1990s.

Note that the regulator could get it wrong by setting too severe a price cap (a high –X figure), which causes company profits to fall and discourages investment in the industry. The utility is likely to react by cutting customer services and employment levels. Once again, government intervention fails to allocate resources efficiently.

Time lags

Markets are increasingly subject to rapid change due to the forces of new technology and globalisation. The availability of information on the internet means that firms can respond to price signals in the market more quickly and efficiently.

However, the government is slow to adapt to these changes because it is subject to a set of rules and regulations, known as 'red tape'. Consequently, it could take years to create the necessary legislation for carrying out important economic projects, e.g the proposed high-speed rail link between London and Folkestone (along the Channel tunnel route) or the construction of a new nuclear reactor at Sizewell, Suffolk. Other examples include the proposed deep-water port at Dibden Bay, Southampton and the expansion of Heathrow Airport through building a new passenger terminal.

Various time-consuming planning enquiries have to be undertaken before major projects get the go-ahead. This may lead to underinvestment in the physical infra-structure of the economy, reducing inward investment and UK international competitiveness. Some economists argue that the government is too inflexible in responding to the growing needs of producers and consumers.

Examination skills and concepts
- Explaining how a lack of market information may cause the government to set taxes and subsidies at too high or too low a level, and so failing to reach the social optimum position.
- Explaining how government intervention distorts the operation of market forces.

For example, maximum and minimum price schemes; buffer stock policies; tax and benefit schemes.

- Recognising how government objectives of equity and environment management may conflict with economic efficiency.

Common examination errors

- Making the answers too 'political' which tends to undermine the economic issues.
- Confusion of market failure with government failure.

Links with other topics

- Agricultural, housing and labour markets (Unit 1).
- Regulatory capture (Unit 4).
- Benefit and tax credits (Unit 3).
- Conflict in government economic objectives (Unit 6).

Questions
&
Answers

This section includes six data-response questions designed to be a key learning, revision and exam preparation resource. They are similar in structure and style to the formal Unit 2 exam paper.

Students can use the questions to reinforce their understanding of the specification subject matter and as practice for completing work under test conditions.

This section includes:
- A student answer of grade-A to grade-C standard for each question.
- Examiner's comments on each student's answer, explaining, where relevant, how the answer could be improved and a higher grade achieved. These comments are preceded by the icon *e*.

Question 1

Postal services in the UK

Postal services will continue to make losses of £1.2 million a day for the next 3 years, according to the Royal Mail's incoming chairman Allan Leighton. This is a world away from the 1990s when the Post Office was a profitable business. The sudden reversal of fortunes can be traced back to rapidly increasing costs, increasing competition, the emergence of substitutes and poor industrial relations. The organisation is in turmoil and the future looks bleak.

Government plans to pay benefits directly into customer bank accounts will mean closure for thousands of sub-post offices as they lose a large proportion of their business. Already, more than 2,000 local post offices close down each year.

Another threat comes from the postal regulator, Graham Corbett of Postcomm, who intends to abolish the letter delivery monopoly enjoyed by the Royal Mail. Currently, any firm intending to provide a letter delivery service is legally obliged to charge a minimum of £1 per letter. However, legal protection for the Royal Mail is to be scrapped by 2007, creating full competition in the market.

Foreign companies also continue to make inroads into the Royal Mail's parcel business (Parcel Force), one of the first to be deregulated in Europe and whose losses are running at £94 million per year. This is a worrying trend, since by 2010 the internet is likely to dominate the purchase method for goods, which will involve a massive increase in deliveries. Parcel Force may not be in a position to invest sufficiently to benefit from this predicted growth in business. The Australian company TNT and the German firm Deutsche Post are poised to increase their UK market share.

Competition also comes from e-mail, text messaging and mobile telephone calls, which are faster and often cheaper than letter deliveries.

However, the postal services are fighting back. In July 2002, the Chairman Allan Leighton decided to ditch the name 'Consignia' and revert back to its strong brand image of the 'Royal Mail'. He also axed 17,000 jobs and abandoned second deliveries in a bid to increase efficiency. Mr Leighton is also seeking permission from the regulator to increase the price of first-class and second-class stamps in order to reduce losses. At the moment 1p is lost on every letter delivered.

The Royal Mail is keen to improve industrial relations among Britain's most strike-prone workforce. Its directors are considering the introduction of a performance-related employee share incentive scheme that could be worth up to £1,000 per year to each postman.

data-response question 1

> The government has failed Royal Mail: over the past decade directors had insufficient investment funds and insufficient independence to make effective business decisions, despite the market gradually being opened up to competition. Pressure is on the government to allow £1.8 billion of accumulated past dividends and cash held in reserves to be made available to the Royal Mail for investment purposes.
>
> Opening up the postal market to competition is a risky business, which does not guarantee improved service for consumers. Some economists claim that letter delivery is a natural monopoly benefiting from huge economies of scale. It will be difficult for the Royal Mail to provide a universal postal service as new entrants 'cherry-pick' the most lucrative areas, namely, business mail and urban delivery services. It could also put an end to the cross-subsidisation between urban and rural post and endanger thousands of jobs. The price of letters is likely to vary considerably between carriers across the UK, leading to confusion among the public.

(a) (i) **Despite enjoying monopoly status in letter delivery services, the Royal Mail is making a loss of £1.2 million per day and the future looks bleak. How might this situation be explained?** (10 marks)

(ii) Discuss measures the Royal Mail could undertake to reduce its losses. (6 marks)

(b) Using your own knowledge and with reference to the extract above, explain the types of entry barriers that are likely to exist for a firm considering entering the UK postal service market. (8 marks)

(c) The extract states that 'the government has failed the Royal Mail'. To what extent do you agree or disagree with this statement? (6 marks)

(d) Examine two advantages and two disadvantages that might exist for consumers in breaking up the Royal Mail's letter delivery monopoly. (10 marks)

■ ■ ■

Candidate's answer

(a) (i) A monopoly refers to a firm which has 25% or more share of a market. The Royal Mail letter delivery service is a good example of a monopoly, where the firm has almost a 100% market share. Despite this, the extract points to huge losses being made due to 'rapidly increasing costs, increasing competition, the emergence of substitutes and poor industrial relations'.

The rising costs could be due to higher fuel prices for delivering mail or higher wages for postal staff. It could also reflect the cost of providing a high-quality service which includes two deliveries per day. Perhaps the directors failed to pay sufficient attention to their costs.

The increasing competition probably comes from private companies setting up and specialising in niche markets, for example, parcel delivery firms or business courier services. They probably cost more than the Royal Mail but are able to charge premium prices. The emergence of substitutes include e-mail, text messaging, mobile phones and faxes. As technology develops, new and better means of communication seem to be inevitable. Both greater competition and substitutes have taken potential custom away from the Royal Mail.

Postal staff have also been the most militant workers in the UK over recent years. The strike action has affected the quality of deliveries and probably caused some customers to go elsewhere. Staff morale is likely to be low, leading to low productivity. All these factors could account for big losses made.

The future looks bleak because of the sheer size of losses being made — £1.2 million per day. This would be more than enough to bankrupt all but the largest of organisations. **7/10 marks**

e There are two parts to this question: why the Royal Mail is making huge losses and why its future prospects are bleak. This is likely to be a common format for data-response questions.

The candidate focuses on the reasons for the losses made by the Royal Mail and draws on a key sentence from the extract. Several points are developed, which show the importance of watching the television news and reading good-quality newspapers to keep up to date with current affairs.

To gain full marks it is necessary to explain in more detail why the future looks grim for the organisation. For example, the government intends to pay benefits directly into customer bank accounts rather than through post offices, thereby reducing revenue. Another threat comes from the newly created regulator for the industry which intends to scrap the legal protection afforded to the Royal Mail's letter delivery services. This has already occurred in the parcel delivery sector, where large losses are being made by the Royal Mail's Parcel Force.

(ii) Drastic measures need to be taken to reduce the Royal Mail's massive losses, especially on the costs side. This will probably require even more redundancies than the 17,000 announced by the new chairman. Scrapping the second daily post and allowing the first post to be delivered after 9 a.m. suggest that the chairman is focusing on cost reductions.

Losses could also be reduced by improving industrial relations so that staff are less likely to strike and more likely to accept new working conditions, leading to greater efficiency. Performance-related pay could also be a step in the right direction as indicated in the extract. **4/6 marks**

e The candidate develops two ideas reasonably well. However, more detail for the two points or three points explained reasonably well would lead to full marks. Other ideas that the candidate could have developed include: the change in the name of the postal service from 'Consignia' to the 'Royal Mail' to create confidence among service users; an increased provision of funds to invest in new equipment and technology which will enable the Royal Mail to compete effectively in the

market, especially as the internet offers new opportunities in goods deliveries; consideration of the revenue side of the business, discussing the pros and cons of higher stamp prices.

(b) Entry barriers are obstacles that make it difficult for firms to enter a market. Entry barriers come in many different forms, for example, control of market outlets as in the case of motor vehicle companies controlling their dealers — dictating who will be allowed to sell their cars and in what price range.

Entry barriers also come from control of raw materials — often the case with precious minerals such as palladium, gold and diamonds. Existing producers may form a cartel and prevent new firms from entering the industry by having a monopoly over supplies.

The most obvious entry barrier to postal services is the government regulation that only allows the Royal Mail to charge less than £1 for a standard letter delivery. All other firms must charge at least £1 per letter. The extract suggests this legal protection is likely to remain until 2007, after which the regulator intends to scrap the charge and issue more licences to enable other firms to enter the bulk mail market. **2/8 marks**

e Unfortunately, the candidate has fallen into the trap of providing a lot of knowledge without being selective over what is and what is not relevant and so has not answered the question set. The only relevant section to the candidate's answer is the last paragraph.

A good answer would focus on postal services as required by the question. A relevant barrier to entry is the strong brand name held by the 'Royal Mail', which could make life very difficult for new firms to gain market share. After 150 years of service the Post Office is well known, trusted and has customer loyalty and experience in abundance. Moreover, incoming firms might have to spend a large sum on advertising to increase customer awareness of their existence in the market. There are also high capital start-up costs, involving sorting offices, postal vehicles, sophisticated machinery and the positioning of post boxes for customer convenience. These capital requirements are expensive and time-consuming to put in place.

(c) The government has 'failed' Royal Mail since it appears to have limited the organisation's ability to use funds for investment purposes. For many years the Post Office was highly profitable and the government accumulated large surpluses, which it directed to other areas of the economy. According to the extract, around £1.8 billion of cash reserves and dividends exist. The lack of investment has reduced the ability of the Post Office to meet the challenges of new technology and growing competition.

The government also limited the powers of Royal Mail directors so that they could not make independent business decisions despite being in a competitive market. For example, several years ago Royal Mail wanted to purchase the Australian parcel carrier TNT to complement Parcel Force but could not do so under government rules. The government also controls the price of postal deliveries, and the extract points to the problem of Royal Mail losing 1p on every letter delivered. This implies the price of stamps has been set too low. **6/6 marks**

e The question asks the candidate to evaluate the effects of government intervention in postal services. Therefore, the examiner wants a value judgement followed by economic reasoning. The candidate develops ideas from the extract critically and shows how government intervention could fail, reducing further the efficiency of a market. Of course, it could be argued that government intervention has made postal services perform better than if they had been left totally to market forces. Postal deliveries are still relatively cheap, simple to follow and uniform throughout the UK. Either argument is valid and could achieve full marks.

(d) One advantage to consumers of breaking up the postal monopoly is that it could lead to more competition. This forces firms to increase efficiency in order to survive. Prices should then fall for consumers, raising their consumer surplus. A second advantage is the increase in choice for consumers. They could pick and choose the delivery service which suited them best. Indeed, we could expect a whole range of new services to be offered as firms tried to differentiate their product and improve quality. There might be two or more letter deliveries per day or even a same day service available.

However, ending the Royal Mail monopoly could lead to a loss of economies of scale as the number of letters delivered by the organisation falls. This is shown in the diagram below where daily letter deliveries fall from 80 million to 60 million, increasing unit costs from OP_1 to OP_2. The firm would be under great pressure to increase postage prices in order to cover the higher unit costs and so consumers could expect to lose out.

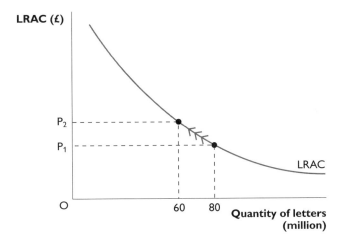

7/10 marks

e The candidate examines two advantages but just one disadvantage for consumers following the loss of Royal Mail's letter monopoly. The question states clearly that *two* advantages and *two* disadvantages should be considered. The candidate might have run out of time, but overall the quality of economic analysis is good.

A second disadvantage that might arise for consumers is the loss of a simplified and uniform national delivery service. It is likely that there would be different prices for sending a letter according to which part of the UK it was to be delivered to. This would cause some confusion and inconvenience to customers. Households and businesses located in rural areas would be likely to suffer most from an expensive and irregular service as cross-subsidisation is ended. The Royal Mail would have to take drastic action to cut its losses and meet the threat of increased competition — the outcome being drastic cuts to the quality of its services.

Scored 26/40 = grade B

Question 2

The UK tobacco market

Extract 1

Tobacco is a heavily taxed product in the UK. This is justified on public health grounds as it helps discourage consumption, especially among young people with relatively low incomes. The UK is also experiencing the most rapid decrease in the world in premature deaths from tobacco smoking among the middle aged. Annual smoking-related deaths fell from over 80,000 in 1965 to less than 40,000 in 1995. This has positive implications for health care and employment.

The decline in tobacco consumption is not just down to high taxes; changing lifestyles, greater public awareness of its dangers, the development of alternatives and the ban on smoking in many public and work places are all having an effect.

However, there is no room for complacency — smoking costs the NHS over £1.7 billion per year and the downward trend in smoking appears to be tailing off. The number of tax-free illegal cigarettes smuggled into the UK continues to grow, creating a black market. One in three cigarettes smoked now avoid taxes at a cost of around £4 billion in lost tax revenue last year. The Tobacco Manufacturers' Association claims this is evidence of government failure.

The government's proposed ban on tobacco advertising and sponsorship may be ineffective as tobacco firms are likely to find other ways of promoting their brands, for example, through the sale of sports equipment, clothing, whisky and travel.

Extract 2

The concentration of market power in the UK tobacco industry is enormous, where three firms supply more than 90% of the market. This has important implications for consumers, producers and the government. The amount of competition in a market affects choice, quality and price, as well as profits, efficiency, innovation and ease of entry.

Table 1 UK cigarette sales

Year	Cigarettes (million)
1991	95,900
1996	81,360
2001	55,723

Source: *Tobacco Manufacturers' Association.*

ata-response question 2

Table 2 Price and tax burden on a packet of 20 cigarettes

Year	Price (£)	Tax (£)
1991	1.80	1.31
1996	2.89	2.26
2001	4.22	3.37

Source: *Tobacco Manufacturers' Association.*

Figure 1 The UK tobacco market in 2000 (% of sales)

Source: *Gallaher's Tobacco Category Review 2001.*

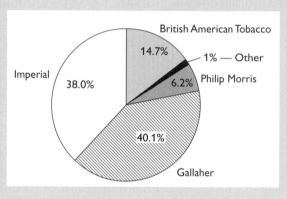

(a) (i) With reference to Table 1, calculate the percentage decline in cigarette sales in the UK between 1991 and 2001. (2 marks)

(ii) Apart from high indirect taxes, how might one account for the decline in cigarette sales over the period? (8 marks)

(b) (i) With reference to Table 2, calculate the tax on a packet of 20 cigarettes as a percentage of its price for 1991 and 2001. (2 marks)

(ii) Examine the reasons why high levels of taxation have been imposed on cigarettes. (8 marks)

(c) Suggest factors which limit the effectiveness of government policies for reducing cigarette consumption. (8 marks)

(d) With reference to Extract 2 and Figure 1, discuss the significance of the concentration of market power for tobacco consumers, tobacco producers and the Competition Commission. (12 marks)

■ ■ ■

Candidate's answer

(a) (i) The percentage decline in cigarette sales between 1991 and 2001 is:

$$\frac{\text{the change in cigarette sales 1991–2001}}{\text{the original cigarette sales in 1991}} \times 100$$

$$\frac{95,900m - 55,723m}{95,900m} \times 100 = 41.9\%$$

1/2 marks

e The calculations are correct but the answer should be **−41.9%**. The minus sign is missing from the answer and so only 1 of the 2 marks would be awarded.

(ii) Apart from high indirect taxes, the decline in cigarette sales is due to changing lifestyles, greater public awareness of the dangers of smoking, the development of alternatives and the ban on smoking in public places.

Changing lifestyles have meant that people are far more health conscious these days and so are more likely to be members of a gym and undertake exercise regularly — this is the opposite of a lifestyle which involves smoking. This change of lifestyle also reflects the increased leisure time and incomes of many people. They have more time and money to spend on things other than cigarettes. Cigarettes may even be regarded as an inferior good.

There is greater public awareness of the dangers of tobacco smoking, due to health education campaigns in schools and doctors' surgeries as well as government-sponsored national adverts on television. The anti-smoking pressure group 'Ash' (Action on Smoking and Health) has also helped to raise and maintain public awareness of the harm brought about by smoking. There is even a national anti-smoking day.

The development of alternatives to smoking (i.e. substitutes) has also helped people to kick the habit. These include nicotine patches and gum, plastic pipes and even tablets available on prescription to help reduce the craving. As long as the price of these substitutes is not too high and people are determined to give up smoking, we can expect to see some effect on tobacco sales.

8/8 marks

e This is a good answer; the candidate extends relevant points from the extract well. Three points, well explained, are sufficient to gain full marks. Remember, data-response questions test more than just comprehension, and this answer shows the importance of using your knowledge of current affairs to develop your answers effectively.

(b) (i) The tax as a percentage of market price of cigarettes in 1991 was:

$$\frac{£1.31}{£1.80} \times 100 = 72.8\%$$

For the year 2001 it was:

$$\frac{£3.37}{£4.22} \times 100 = 79.9\%$$

There has been an increase in tax as a percentage of market price from 72.8% to 79.9%. **2/2 marks**

e The candidate has calculated the percentage increase correctly.

(ii) The government has imposed high taxes on cigarettes due to the harm they cause people. The extract refers to young people not being able to afford cigarettes because of the high taxes and so discouraging youngsters from taking up the habit. It also mentions that fewer middle-aged people smoke and so less of them die from related diseases. This means less money is required to spend on treating smokers in hospitals and more people will be in employment. **3/8 marks**

e This answer promises much but fails to deliver. The key instruction is for candidates to 'examine' the reason for high taxes on cigarettes. It is the most testing part of the data-response exercise and is where marks are often lost.

The candidate identifies some of the relevant information from the text but fails to develop it fully. A more effective answer would link the high cigarette taxes to high prices relative to young people's incomes. One might also consider that demand is likely to be price sensitive for young people just starting to smoke — making the high tax policy more effective. If fewer young people take up smoking it means the overall customer base for tobacco companies will fall rapidly as many existing smokers will die prematurely.

Consideration could also be given to the high percentage of 15- and 16-year-olds who smoke. Would the figures be worse if taxes were lower or do they suggest that the high taxation policy is a failure? Candidates need to demonstrate that they are examining the policy.

The health-care argument could also be handled better. Fewer smokers would mean that National Health Service resources could be reallocated to other areas of health care, e.g. care of elderly patients, treatment of kidney disease. The health minister mentions the financial cost to the NHS is £1.7 billion per year. It is clear that an opportunity cost exists for the treatment of smoking-related diseases within the NHS and the candidate could make use of this.

The reasons attached to employment should also be explained properly. Fewer smokers would lead to a healthier and larger workforce, which in turn would result in higher productivity and income. Furthermore, fewer working days would be lost through illness and there may be lower labour recruitment costs for firms.

Finally, the candidate could explain that cigarette smoking is a market failure for two reasons: first, it is a demerit good, yielding greater disutility to consumers than they actually believe to be the case; second, there are negative externalities involved for the health-care services, employers and passive smokers. The latter argument could include an external cost diagram. The government imposes the high taxes in an attempt to correct market failure. Two reasons, examined well, should enable candidates to achieve full marks.

(c) Many smokers buy cigarettes on the black market. This is where cigarettes are sold illegally without UK taxes being imposed and so are at a much lower price. Around one in three cigarettes are from the black market and this costs the government £4 billion in lost tax revenue. The lower price of illegal cigarettes encourages people to smoke.

Another reason why government policies to reduce cigarette consumption might not be very effective is because tobacco is an addictive good and so people will still buy it even at high prices. It is a drug — people get addicted to the nicotine in cigarettes. **5/8 marks**

e In this answer the candidate identifies one problem from the text — a growth of the black market. This point is developed to include an explanation of a black market and why it leads to cheaper cigarettes.

The candidate raises a second limitation not mentioned in the extract explicitly — tobacco being an addictive product and, consequently, price inelastic in demand. This is a good point to raise and illustrates how data-response questions can be used as a launch pad for developing further ideas. This shows how important it is to understand the scope of the question. If the candidate had introduced a diagram-matic treatment of the second point, such as the following, full marks would have been achieved.

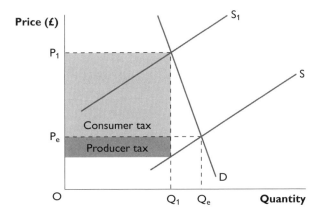

High indirect taxes may only lead to a relatively small fall in cigarette consumption.

A further point which the candidate could raise is how tobacco firms may get around advertising bans, reducing the effectiveness of government policies. They appear to be diversifying into different markets, but keeping the same brand names as for their tobacco products, e.g. Lucky Strike clothing, John Player Special Whisky and Kent Travel.

(d) There are three big firms dominating the cigarette market in the UK, which implies less choice and high prices for consumers. There might not be much competition

ata-response question 2

in the industry. The three largest firms, Gallagher, Imperial and BAT, have a combined market share of 92.8%. The tobacco firms may be reluctant to compete over price and instead look at other forms of competition, such as quality of tobacco, advertising and packaging. There might even be the possibility of collusion occurring, though this would be difficult to prove. The Competition Commission might have to investigate the industry to see if any collusion is going on.

6/12 marks

This is a reasonable answer in which the candidate uses the data from Figure 1. Overall, the candidate needs to extend some of the points made. For example, the candidate might suggest that price competition is not desirable when demand for the product is price inelastic. Price cuts would lead to a fall in total revenue. Another relevant point is that the tobacco firms produce many different brands of cigarettes in order to provide more choice for consumers, but also to develop brand loyalty. The wide choice of brands might mislead consumers into thinking that the tobacco market is a highly competitive one.

More is also required on the role of the Competition Commission. This organisation is more likely to investigate markets when there is a high concentration of production among just a few firms. Its main role is to ensure that the firms are competing against each other and not involved in restrictive trade practices, such as price fixing, allocation of market shares and the creation of entry barriers. The Competition Commission is likely to keep an eye on profits as a percentage of sales and assets for each company to make sure they are not too excessive, as this would imply collusion was occurring.

Scored 25/40 = high grade C

Question 3

The North Sea fishing industry

Extract 1 Declining fish stocks

There used to be 2 million tonnes of mackerel swimming in the North Sea and even more herring. For centuries they supported communities all around the coastal areas of Europe. Annual catches of 1 million tonnes were common but they gradually dropped to nothing. Mackerel are now commercially extinct. Cod, haddock, hake, plaice, sole, whiting and prawns are going the same way. The sea has lost its former abundance and the end may loom for commercial fishing.

The decline in North Sea fish stocks is the result of a 'free-for-all' in the market leading to a modern fishing boom. Furthermore, improvements in technology allowed boats to fish in fog and locate shoals of fish within 50 feet. There are also more vessels tracking the fish — the largest in the world is the Irish registered *Atlantic Dawn* which has nets twice the size of the Millennium Dome.

Global warming has also played a part. Rising sea temperatures have caused a reduction in the levels of plankton, the basic foodstuff in our oceans for many creatures. Small and large fish are doomed to extinction.

Extract 2 Fish quotas

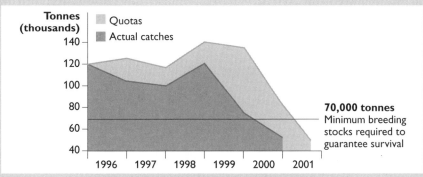

Figure 1 North Sea cod catches and quotas

The European Commission has introduced quotas to save the cod. A quota is a quantitative limit on the amount of fish which can be caught. Last year British fishermen were restricted to a quota of 34,000 tonnes but only caught 24,000 tonnes. More than 80% of the cod caught is below breeding age; instead of 5-foot monsters, cod are now just inches long.

ata-response question 3

One of the greatest scandals of the past 25 years has been the practice of discarding undersized dead fish back into the sea and catching bigger ones to get full value out of the quota system. Clearly, it makes sense to increase the mesh size of nets so that small fish below the official size permitted are not caught.

Adapted from 'Overfishing brings more bad news to struggling ports' by Paul Brown, *Guardian*, 15 December 2000.

Extract 3 Fish farming

Fish produced in farms currently account for over one quarter of all fish directly consumed by humans. More than 220 species of shellfish and finfish are farmed, producing over 29 million tonnes per year. Many believe that this growth has relieved pressure from natural fish stocks as well as creating thousands of jobs, both directly and indirectly, in remote communities.

However, fish farming does have its critics: an average of 1.9 kilograms of wild fish is required to feed 1.0 kilogram of farmed fish, raising questions of efficiency. Disease also thrives in densely populated farms which can contaminate local wild fish. Uneaten food, fish faeces and antibiotics are regularly flushed into surrounding waters. Furthermore, when large numbers escape from captivity the natural gene pool is distorted.

Source: 'Fish crisis', *Guardian*, Special Report 25 November 2001.

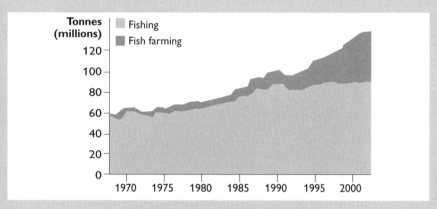

Figure 2 Growth of fish farming

Source: *EU Fisheries Report*, 2001

(a) **With reference to Extract 1 and other sources, discuss reasons for the decline in North Sea fish stocks.** (10 marks)

(b) **Examine the likely economic effects of a collapse in North Sea fish stocks for consumers and producers.** (8 marks)

(c) (i) **With reference to Extract 2 and using a supply and demand diagram, explain how EU quotas are expected to reduce fish catches in the North Sea.** (6 marks)

(ii) **With reference to Figure 1, explain why the decline in North Sea fisheries is an example of government failure.** (6 marks)

(d) (i) **With reference to Extract 3, identify two external costs and two external benefits from the growth in fish farming.** (2 marks)

(ii) **Using a diagram, explain how the social optimum price and output position differs from that determined through market forces for farmed fish.** (8 marks)

■ ■ ■

Candidate's answer

(a) Fish stocks have declined because of the 'free-for-all' in the market. This indicates a lack of regulation of fishing and so too many fish have been caught over the years. In addition, improvements in technology mean the boats are better equipped to locate and catch the fish. Furthermore, the extract suggests there has been a big increase in the number of fishing boats, along with their size — the *Atlantic Dawn* being a good example of the latter. There are now too many boats trying to catch too few fish. **5/10 marks**

> ℮ The candidate identifies the relevant points from the extract but needs to extend them further; it is not just a comprehension exercise. For example, the candidate recognises the lack of regulation of fish catches in the past but fails to link this to the lack of property rights over the seas and oceans. If no one owns the seas then it is in each fisherman's interest to catch the fish before someone else does. Self-interest prevails but it eventually leads to exhaustion of fish stocks. In this case, the lack of ownership rights is a market failure.
>
> The candidate is also asked to discuss other factors not mentioned directly in the extract which help to explain the decline in fish stocks. This could include reference to the increase in pollution of our seas or the introduction of fish quotas in recent years.

(b) The likely economic effects of a collapse in North Sea fish stocks will be harmful for both consumers and producers. Consumers are likely to experience higher fish prices and so reduce their demand. Some fish producers are likely to close down and lay off staff as their profits turn into losses. This is not just for the fishing boats but also in other related businesses such as boat-building, net-making, canning factories and fish and chip shops. There might be a type of negative multiplier effect on the fish industry. It could be very harmful for major fishing ports such as Fleetwood and Grimsby. **5/8 marks**

> ℮ This is an unbalanced answer. The candidate 'examines' the likely effects on producers very well, but has little to say about the effects for consumers. 4 marks would be gained for examining fish producers, but only 1 mark for consideration of consumers. It is important to try to provide balance in your answers. To gain full marks the

ata-response question 3

candidate could have explored how consumer choice would be affected and how fish might even become a type of luxury good. Consumers might also switch to substitute goods such as red meat or poultry, but these are not close alternatives.

(c) (i) An EU quota is a quantitative limit on fish catches. The effect should be to decrease supply of fish and so drive up its price. This is shown in the diagram where supply shifts from S_1 to S_2, and price rises from OP_1 to OP_2. The quota is drawn as a vertical supply curve since only a certain amount of fish can be caught, no matter what the price is. The demand curve for fish is shown to be quite price inelastic since many regard it as a basic food product.

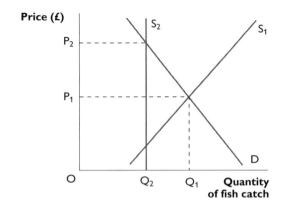

6/6 marks

e This is a sound answer in which the candidate uses correct diagrammatic analysis and explores the issue of elasticity.

(ii) The decline in North Sea fish stocks is a type of government failure since the imposition of quotas appears to be ineffective in protecting fish stocks. Ever since quotas were introduced in 1996, they have exceeded the actual amount of fish caught. This is shown by Figure 1 and means that the quotas have been set at too high a level, probably to keep the fishing industry happy. At the same time, the European Commission can claim to have done something to protect fish stocks by having quotas.
4/6 marks

e This is a promising answer and the candidate makes use of Figure 1. Some mention could have been made of the minimum level of breeding stocks required to guarantee survival. In Figure 1 this is shown to be 70,000 tonnes. However, it appears that the fish quota was only set at this level in 2001. To gain full marks the candidate needed to mention a second type of government failure. For example, output restrictions have led to the problem of discarding dead undersized fish back into the sea in order to leave room on the fishermen's quotas to catch bigger ones and earn more money. Perhaps the government has failed to increase the official mesh size of nets to help protect future stocks. The government may also have failed to allocate sufficient resources to protecting fish stocks and monitoring the catches landed at various ports around the UK.

(d) (i) Two external costs are the spread of disease within densely populated fish farms which could adversely affect the local wild population and how the natural gene pool is distorted when large numbers of fish escape from captivity. Two external benefits include the removal of pressure from natural fish populations and the creation of thousands of jobs in remote communities.

2/2 marks

ℓ A neat answer — the candidate avoids wasting time as just 2 marks are available.

(ii) The social optimum price and output position is where total social costs equal total social benefits. This is shown to be at price OP_1 and quantity OQ_1 in the diagram. The market determined optimum only takes into account private costs and benefits from an economic activity. This is shown to be at price OP_e and quantity OQ_e.

If external benefits of fish farming are greater than its external costs, we would expect to see the social optimum quantity exceed the market determined optimum quantity as shown in the diagram. This may well be the case since the government often gives planning permission for new fish farms. There has been a large increase in fish farming over the past 10 years, shown by Figure 2.

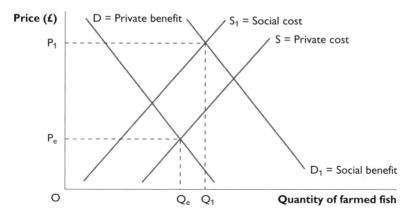

5/8 marks

ℓ The candidate makes the mistake of referring to total social costs and benefits rather than marginal social costs and benefits. The social optimum position will be where the social cost of producing the last unit just equals the social benefit gained from consuming it. This will yield the maximum net social benefit (total social benefit minus total social cost). The same principle applies to identifying where the market determined optimum position is (the private cost of producing the last unit just equals the private benefit gained from its consumption).

However, the rest of the answer is good and the candidate applies it to the fish farm industry effectively.

Scored 27/40 = grade B

Question 4

Terminal 5: Heathrow Airport

In November 2001, after the longest ever planning inquiry in the UK lasting almost 4 years, the government approved plans to build a new terminal at London Heathrow Airport. Completion of Terminal 5 is expected by 2007 with construction costs rising to £2 billion. Traffic at Heathrow, Europe's busiest airport, is expected to grow from its current 57 million to 87 million passengers per year by 2013, holding off the competitive threat offered by other key airports at Paris, Frankfurt and Amsterdam. Demand is expected to continue to grow due to rising real incomes and the increase in business traffic. Greater price competition between carriers and more choice of destinations are further reasons for robust growth.

Supporters of Terminal 5 claim that increasing the capacity of Heathrow will make best use of the airport's existing infrastructure and land (nearly 3,000 acres already in the perimeter fence). The terminal will be built on a disused sewage works causing minimal impact on wildlife. Heathrow is the most popular destination among air carriers and passengers in the southeast. The project will also create 6,000 construction jobs and a further 12,000 in operation services. Heathrow is already an important employment centre with 68,000 on-airport jobs and a further 245,000 people employed indirectly.

A report by the top accounting firm, Coopers & Lybrand, identified further benefits from Terminal 5. Inward investment and foreign tourism into the UK will grow more quickly, leading to an extra £2 billion of income per year.

Figure 1 shows the projected increase in demand and capacity (with and without construction of Terminal 5) for air travel in the southeast of England to 2010. Even with the new terminal at Heathrow, supply is unlikely to keep up with demand, leading to higher prices and the diversion of traffic abroad to other airports.

However, serious concerns have been raised by the green pressure group Friends of the Earth. It points to Terminal 5 being the largest ever structure to be built on green-belt land — the building alone will be more than twice the size of Wembley Stadium. It believes this is just the start of further encroachment into green-belt land — a new runway is likely to be required and then there are housing and business needs. There will also be more noise and air pollution and pressure to increase the number of night flights.

Serious implications exist for road transport in the area, already the most congested in the whole of the UK. Plans are under way to widen the M25 to 12 lanes and to build a new spur road from the motorway to the airport. The airport authority intends to provide a further 21,500 car parking spaces to cater for an extra 49,000 car journeys each day to and from Heathrow. This is on top of extending the underground tube network and overland rail link.

Friends of the Earth claims the projected growth in air traffic demand for southeast England is wildly exaggerated. It believes the figures have been deliberately inflated to justify construction and do not take into account factors which might limit demand in the near future, for example, the threat of air terrorism, a global recession, increased oil prices and mergers between air carriers.

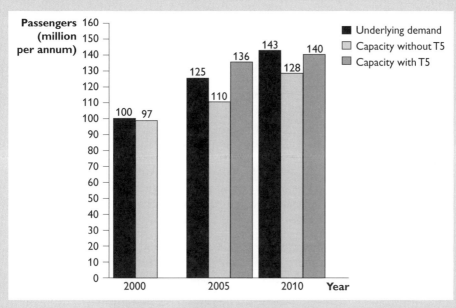

Figure 1 Air passenger demand and capacity for southeast England — projected growth

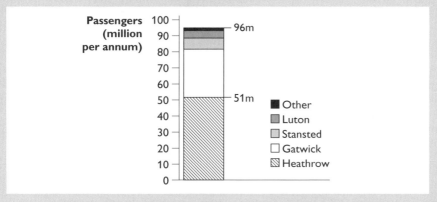

Figure 2 Air passengers for the London airports in 1997

Source: British Airways — Terminal 5 (**www.britishairways.com**).

data-response question 4

(a) Discuss possible reasons for the projected growth in air traffic demand in southeast England as shown in Figure 1. (12 marks)

(b) (i) With reference to Figure 2, calculate the percentage of air traffic in southeast England handled by Heathrow Airport in 1997. (2 marks)

(ii) Suggest reasons why the government decided not to choose an alternative plan of massive expansion at one or more of the other airports serving London and the southeast. (6 marks)

(c) Using diagrammatic analysis, explain the likely external costs and benefits from the construction and operation of Terminal 5. (12 marks)

(d) Examine why the projected growth in demand for air traffic may be inaccurate. (8 marks)

■ ■ ■

Candidate's answer

(a) According to Figure 1, air traffic demand was approximately 100 million passengers in southeast England during the year 2000. This is expected to increase to over 140 million passengers by 2010. The projected growth in air traffic demand for southeast England is due to a number of reasons.

Firstly, there are rising real incomes and so people can afford to travel by air more to take holidays. Demand for holiday travel is generally regarded as income elastic. It is also likely that the increased incomes have been accompanied by more leisure time and so people have more time for holidays these days.

A second reason is due to the growth of businesses and their increasing international links. More and more firms today trade overseas, where they may have important export markets or imported equipment and raw materials. It is part of globalisation as trade barriers fall and cheaper fuel boosts the demand for air travel.

A third reason is due to the fierce price competition between airline carriers. New entrants such as Go and Ryanair have contributed to a price war which has seen some fares fall to as low as 1p! Under these circumstances, people find it cheaper to holiday overseas than at home in the UK.

A fourth point is that the new entrants have increased the choice of destinations and the frequency of flights. It is as if the new capacity has created the demand for air travel. Moreover, we are bombarded with adverts of exotic holidays, together with tourist television programmes that encourage us to fly away for a break from the miserable weather. **12/12 marks**

e This is a very good answer. The candidate begins by discussing the data shown in Figure 1 and then develops points from the extract using economic analysis. There are at least four main strands of thinking and this would be sufficient to gain full marks (3 marks for each strand).

(b) (i) Heathrow airport had 53.1% of all air traffic in southeast England in 1997.

$$\frac{51 \text{ million}}{96 \text{ million}} \times 100 = 53.1\%$$

2/2 marks

📝 The candidate has calculated the percentage correctly.

(ii) One reason for not choosing the massive expansion of other airports is because they may be in a weaker position to increase capacity. Most of the expansion at Heathrow airport will take place within its perimeter fence, making better use of its 3,000 acres and disused sewage works. This suggests the cost of buying land and the purchase of buildings in the way is likely to be lower for Heathrow.

The extract also mentions that there will be minimal impact upon wildlife compared to expansion elsewhere. The government and airport authorities are likely to have taken these reduced external costs into account when making their decision. **4/6 marks**

📝 The candidate explains two reasons why expansion at Heathrow was preferred to expansion at any of the other airports in southeast England. Each reason would earn 2 marks, but to gain full marks a third idea is required. For example, Heathrow is a more popular destination for airline companies and passengers than Luton, Stansted and Gatwick. Consequently, Heathrow airport is more likely to attract passenger growth than the other options and so from an economic point of view it makes sense to locate the new terminal at Heathrow.

(c) There are various external costs and benefits associated with the construction of Terminal 5. On the cost side there are problems of noise and air pollution from increasing air and road traffic. We can also expect more road traffic congestion, blocking up nearby motorways. External costs are shown in the following diagram in the shaded area, and represent the difference between private and social costs.

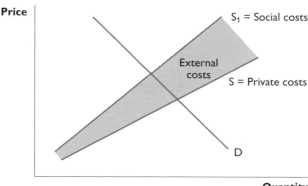

ata-response question 4

The external benefits include the creation of some 6,000 construction jobs and a further 12,000 jobs in operation services. A report by Coopers & Lybrand also reveals that there will be an increase in foreign investment and tourism into the UK as a result of improved air links. External benefits are shown in the following diagram and represent the difference between private and social benefits.

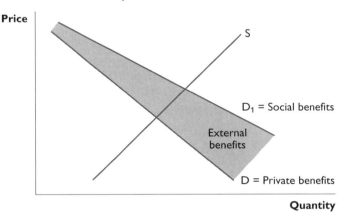

7/12 marks

e The candidate illustrates both external costs and external benefits clearly and understands the meaning of the two concepts (though a definition would make the answer better). The diagrams could be improved by showing the original and new equilibrium price and output positions. It is also more accurate to label the cost and benefit curves with the term 'marginal' (as demonstrated in the Content Guidance section of this guide). The candidate would gain 4/6 marks for the diagrams.

The candidate identifies several types of external costs and benefits but the accompanying explanations are too brief. For example, the problem of increased noise pollution could be expanded to include night flights and local residents' demands for compensation. The candidate could also explain a few more types of external costs and benefits. For example, property prices underneath the flight path are likely to fall and there is a violation of protected green-belt land which could open up the floodgates for more development — the new terminal will increase pressure for an additional runway to be built at Heathrow. In addition, there may be an increase in the danger of accidents through greater use of the already congested skies over southeast England. An external benefit might include the creation of more local businesses to supply services to Terminal 5. The candidate would gain 3 out of 6 marks for this part of the answer.

(d) Friends of the Earth suggests the projected growth in air traffic is wildly exaggerated in order to ensure that Terminal 5 is given government approval. There are vested interests in getting Terminal 5 built, for example, among building contractors and airline carriers. They could gain high profits from the project. In addition, the terrible events of 11 September 2001, where the World Trade Centre towers were destroyed by terrorists, show how vulnerable the airline industry might be to sudden shocks. Several international carriers went bankrupt and others needed government assistance to stay in business due to the downturn in demand in the aftermath of the attacks. **5/8 marks**

e This is a good answer in which the candidate develops two points from the last paragraph of the extract. However, there is room to examine some more ideas, e.g. the possibility of a global recession, rising oil prices and mergers. Mergers between airlines, for example, tend to restrict competition and may even lead to monopoly power on some routes. The price war between airlines is also likely to be temporary and fares will rise eventually, reducing passenger demand. There is growing competition too from other airports such as Paris, Frankfurt and Amsterdam; the growth of these airports could take some custom away from Heathrow. Finally, predicting air travel demand over a long time period is subject to major errors because so many factors could change.

Scored 30/40 = grade A

Question 5

UK health-care provision

The National Health Service (NHS) has provided universal health care, which is free at the point of consumption, for more than 50 years. Many health economists believe it has achieved productive efficiency. Hospital beds are filled within 20 minutes of becoming vacant. Each surgeon performs more operations than ever before whilst nurses have a greater number of patients to look after. Furthermore, the organisation has a highly qualified and well-trained workforce.

However, the NHS is allocatively inefficient. Over the past decade it has come under intense pressure as the increase in demand for state health-care services has consistently outstripped increases in supply. The outcome has been a large rise in hospital waiting lists for operations to over a million people. State health care can no longer be considered a public good, though it remains a merit good.

The growing demand for NHS services is due partly to demographic factors such as an ageing population, but it also reflects improvements in medical knowledge and the treatment of previously untreatable illnesses. The emergence of new diseases and increased public awareness and expectations over the quality of treatment have added to the pressures.

The NHS also faces severe supply restraints; the acute shortage of doctors and nurses has led to some hospital wards remaining closed and NHS managers trying desperately to close the gap through running intensive recruitment campaigns overseas. Furthermore, many hospital buildings are old, dilapidated and unsuitable for health-care use, reflecting a prolonged period of underinvestment in the capital infrastructure.

Health-care budgets have lagged behind their counterparts in other European Union (EU) countries — the UK only spends 6% of its gross domestic product on health care compared to the EU average of 8%. The government is keen to close the gap and NHS expenditure is set to increase by 6% per annum in real terms between the years 2000 and 2004.

Unfortunately, this increased funding will take a long period of time to have any noticeable effect. Some economists believe the time is right for a significant expansion in private health-care provision.

(a) (i) **What is meant by the term 'productive efficiency' and why might the NHS be regarded as having achieved this?** (5 marks)

(ii) **What is meant by the term 'allocative efficiency' and why has the NHS not achieved this?** (5 marks)

(b) Explain why state health care is 'no longer considered to be a public good though it remains a merit good.' (6 marks)

(c) (i) Using supply and demand analysis, explain why there are more than a million people on hospital waiting lists for **NHS** operations. (8 marks)

(ii) Why might improvements in state health-care provision take a long period of time to have any noticeable effect? (6 marks)

(d) Evaluate the advantages and disadvantages to the public of 'a significant expansion in private health-care provision' in the **UK**. (10 marks)

■ ■ ■

Candidate's answer

(a) (i) Productive efficiency refers to an organisation achieving the maximum output from a given quantity of factor inputs. This implies costs per unit of output are minimised. The NHS has achieved productive efficiency since it appears to be fully utilising its resources; for example, the extract refers to a fast turnaround in filling available hospital beds and on average surgeons are carrying out more operations and nurses are looking after more patients. The NHS is using its highly qualified and trained workforce to maximum effect. **5/5 marks.**

e The candidate achieves maximum marks by defining productive efficiency and using the prompts from the extract correctly. There is no need for a diagrammatic treatment to gain full marks here.

(ii) Allocative efficiency is where the cost to an organisation of producing the last unit of output just equals the benefit obtained by the consumer of that unit of output. In other words, the marginal cost to the firm is equated with the marginal benefit gained by the consumer of the last unit of output. One should note that economists assume marginal benefit can be measured by the price a consumer is willing to pay for a good or service.

Allocative efficiency does not appear to have been achieved by the NHS since the price mechanism is restricted; state health-care services are provided free at the point of consumption and so the cost of producing the last unit will exceed the price charged. Unfortunately, this gives rise to an excess demand for health-care services. Some consumers are willing to pay directly for a particular service, for example a hernia operation, but are unable to obtain it on the NHS without joining a lengthy waiting list. They will have to go privately to have the operation. **5/5 marks**

e Again, the candidate achieves maximum marks and recognises that allocative efficiency cannot be achieved when the price mechanism is unable to operate by charging consumers.

(b) State health care is not a public good since it fails to meet the two key criteria, namely, non-exclusion in consumption and non-rivalry in consumption. The fact

data-response question 5

of lengthy hospital waiting lists indicates that consumers compete between each other over the availability of beds and many are excluded, at least for some of the time. Some economists suggest state health care is more like a quasi-public good where the criteria are fulfilled up to a given number of patients, before exclusion and rivalry sets in. Health care is still a merit good since it yields positive externalities.

3/6 marks

e The first part of this answer is excellent and the candidate clearly understands the difference between public and quasi-public goods. However, the second part is too limited and fails to get to the heart of what a merit good actually is. The candidate should define a merit good and then give an example of why health care falls into this category.

(c) (i) The extract mentions that increases in demand for state health care have constantly outstripped increases in supply, the consequence being to cause over a million people to be on hospital waiting lists. This is shown in the following diagram. Demand and supply are originally at D_1 and S_1 respectively. Since health care is provided free of charge, there is an initial excess demand of Q_eQ_1.

However, the increase in demand and supply over recent years has caused both curves to shift to the right, to D_2 and S_2. Since demand has increased faster than supply, the hospital waiting lists have increased — shown by the gap between Q_2 and Q_3, which is greater than the original gap of Q_eQ_1. The supply curve is drawn as a vertical line since there is a fixed amount of funds allocated by the government to the NHS.

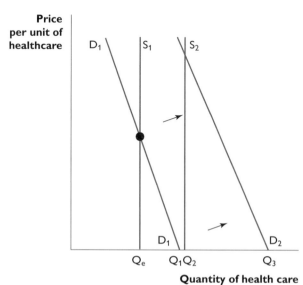

6/8 marks

ℓ This is a good answer. The candidate shifts the supply and demand curves correctly and explains them properly. To gain full marks the candidate also needs to explain one or two reasons for the growth in demand for health care, e.g. the ageing UK population or the improvements in medical knowledge which have made formerly untreatable illnesses treatable, but at great financial cost.

(ii) Improvements in state health-care provision may take a long time before they become noticeable. This might be because of the time-lag between the government announcing increased NHS funding and the actual spending of the extra monies.

Furthermore, the extract indicates there has been serious underinvestment in the capital infrastructure for hospitals and clinics. This backlog of investment could take years to complete, again delaying noticeable improvements to state health-care services.

It also takes several years to train nurses fully and much longer for doctors and surgeons. But this will involve the building of more colleges and courses for training personnel, which could take years to implement. All of the above factors tend to make supply of health services price inelastic.

A final reason why noticeable improvements in state health-care services may take a long time to appear is because of the rapid increase in demand. It means hospitals are struggling just to maintain existing health-care standards — let alone improving them. **6/6 marks**

ℓ Another excellent answer in which the candidate explains four valid points. Two points would have been enough to gain full marks.

(d) There are several arguments in support of increasing private health-care provision for the public. It could lead to an increase in competition between health-care firms, creating more consumer choice and quality of service provision. The use of the price mechanism means services will follow changes in customer demand, leading to allocative efficiency. Private health care should also take some of the strain away from the NHS as wealthier patients can seek treatment in the private sector.

On the other hand, there are several problems arising from an expansion of private health care, notably one of equity. Many people are unable to afford private treatment and so there will be an increase in health-care inequality. The most vulnerable in society are unlikely to obtain private health insurance, for example, unemployed and casual workers, and the sick and elderly.

Another problem is that the public has insufficient medical knowledge to make the best choice over where and from whom to obtain treatment. There could even be a temptation for medical practitioners to 'over treat' people in order to gain more payment.

ata-response question 5

A final problem is the loss of staff from the NHS who may be tempted to work for private health-care firms, where pay and fringe benefits are better. Ironically, this could worsen staff shortages among the NHS trusts and lengthen hospital waiting lists for the public.   **8/10 marks**

Another sound answer, revealing a range of ideas and some evaluation. However, there is a slight imbalance in the candidate's argument, as it is rather brief on the possible benefits to the public of private health-care expansion. These advantages require some evaluation, e.g. is there an increase in competition or is it that existing private health-care firms simply expand to meet growing consumer demand? Will increased competition really lead to improved quality of services and, if so, how is this meant to work? How quickly can private firms respond to changes in consumer demand? After all, staff may require retraining and medical equipment may need to be replaced.

Scored 33/40 = mid grade A

Question 6

The Common Agricultural Policy (CAP)

The European Common Agricultural Policy (CAP) was created more than 40 years ago to increase agricultural productivity, ensure adequate food supplies, stabilise farm prices and raise farm incomes.

There has been bitter criticism of a system which created massive food surpluses, high food prices and more taxes for consumers. The CAP costs each household more than £300 a year.

Under the CAP, EU farmers are given guaranteed minimum prices for cereals, wine and meat, which are set above the free market price. The surpluses are purchased and stored by the government, to be 'dumped' overseas with the help of export subsidies. As the surpluses grew, the government introduced a 'set-aside' policy which pays farmers not to produce on 10–15% of their farmland.

The CAP also has a system of tariffs which block cheap food imports from more efficient producers outside the EU. This has the effect of reducing competition and consumer choice, and prompting a trade war with the United States of America.

The European Commission has failed to overcome market forces. The price support system has encouraged farmers to embrace new technology and increase production as much as possible, paying scant attention to the environment. However, demand for food is virtually static and so the downward pressure on market prices increases the cost of supporting the farmers.

The government is very inefficient in transferring income to farmers. The annual cost to consumers and taxpayers is more than twice the gain in gross income to farmers as hefty payments are made to administrators, storage agencies and export subsidies. Moreover, farmers are faced with higher input costs as they seek to maximise production.

Another glaring problem of the CAP is that payments are linked directly to production, leading to 80% of the farm subsidies going to just 20% of farmers. The small farmers receive very little help compared to the big agricultural producers.

Over the past 2 years, the European Commission has sought to reform the CAP. This involves capping payments made to big farmers and linking aid to managing the countryside rather than to production. Under these proposals, for example, farmers would be paid for maintaining and creating woodlands, hedgerows, wildlife and ponds. Small farmers are likely to gain at the expense of large farmers. Furthermore, the minimum price support systems would gradually be phased out. These reforms are necessary if EU enlargement is to take place without bankrupting the European Commission. Ten countries have applied to join the EU in 2004, most of them with large agricultural sectors.

Source: *Eurostat 2002.*

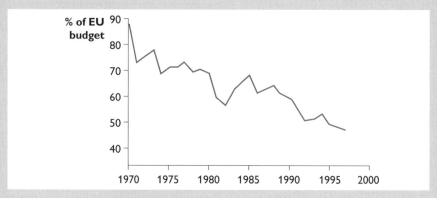

Figure 1 Agricultural expenditure

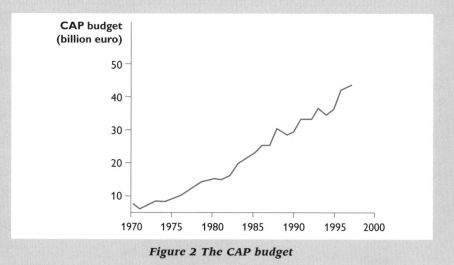

Figure 2 The CAP budget

(a) To what extent do the original reasons for the creation of the **CAP** still apply today? (8 marks)

(b) (i) Using a demand and supply diagram, illustrate and explain how setting a guaranteed minimum price above the free market price has led to grain mountains and wine lakes. (6 marks)

   (ii) Apart from the food and wine surpluses, what evidence in the extract suggests government intervention in European agricultural markets has failed? (6 marks)

(c) (i) How can one explain the apparent contradiction between Figures 1 and 2 in EU government spending on agriculture? (4 marks)

(ii) **Explain why reform of the CAP is a necessary precondition before the enlargement of the European Union can take place.** (4 marks)

(d) **Examine the likely economic effects of the proposed agricultural reforms for EU farmers, consumers and government finances.** (12 marks)

■ ■ ■

Candidate's answer

(a) The European Common Agricultural Policy was created more than 40 years ago to increase agricultural productivity, ensure adequate food supplies, stabilise farm prices and raise farm incomes. However, the CAP has become a victim of its own success. Today, agricultural support costs each household in the EU more than £300 a year. **1/8 marks**

e Unfortunately, the candidate has simply copied the text and has made little effort to elaborate on the reasons or provide a proper value judgement. It is always a bad idea to copy whole chunks of information from the extract, yet it is still quite common for candidates to do this. If you use sentences from the extract, put them in quotation marks and follow them up with a critical comment. You must add value to the information given in the extract.

The candidate would receive 1 mark for stating that the CAP is a victim of its own success, implying that the original reasons for its existence have ended.

A more effective answer could take the following form:

The original reasons for introducing the CAP do not appear valid today. For example, one reason for the introduction of the CAP was to increase agricultural productivity, that is, to increase output per farm and farm worker. Agricultural yields were quite low just after the Second World War and there were fears of food shortages. The government provided incentives for farmers to increase productivity by guaranteeing prices above the market price as well as offering subsidies for the purchase of machinery and fertiliser. The CAP ensured that agricultural output grew faster than Europe's population — so meeting the food requirements. However, today there are very large surpluses which suggest that the CAP has outlived its purpose.

Another reason for setting up the CAP was to prevent wild price fluctuations, a common feature of agricultural markets. This was caused by inelastic demand and erratic seasonal supply, often explained through the cobweb model. However, the CAP guaranteed high, stable prices for agricultural goods as the government purchased food surpluses. This also had the effect of increasing farm incomes. Today, many economists believe the CAP is no longer required — they believe that farm incomes are high enough and that food prices are too high. If the CAP is withdrawn, farmers will be forced to become more efficient in order to maintain their incomes. The price of agricultural goods will fall too, eliminating the surpluses and benefiting consumers.

The £300 annual cost of the CAP to each household is far too high and can no longer be justified.

If candidates are required to make qualitative value judgements, it is possible to develop a contrasting argument in support of the CAP. For example, the CAP may still be necessary to maintain adequate food supplies and protect farm incomes. Without the CAP, many farmers are likely to go out of business and the price of agricultural goods suddenly revert back to wild fluctuations associated with the cobweb cycle. There could also be many job losses in agriculture leading to poverty and rural depopulation.

(b) (i) The diagram shows the introduction of a guaranteed minimum price for grain of OP_2 which causes farmers to raise output to OQ_2 because they can make more profit. However, demand will fall to OQ_1 as it becomes too expensive to buy so much grain. A surplus of Q_1Q_2 is created which is bought up by the government through the guarantee. There is an excess supply. Over time grain mountains and wine lakes will be created, especially since farmers have an incentive to produce as much as possible.

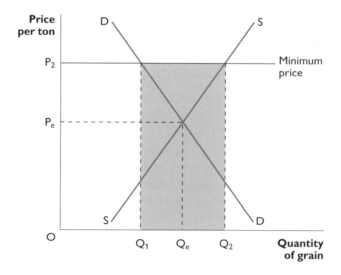

5/6 marks

e The candidate's diagram is correct and applies to the context of grain. The demand and supply curves and axes are labelled correctly. The food surplus is also identified correctly as Q_1Q_2 (although this might be expressed better as $OQ_2–OQ_1$). The shaded area represents total government spending on purchasing the excess supply and adding to its stockpile. When candidates are required to draw a diagram the marks are usually split: half for the diagram and half for the explanation. In this example the candidate would gain full marks for the diagram. However, the explanation could be improved by reference to the original equilibrium price and quantity, and use of the terms 'contraction' in demand and 'expansion' in supply. A comment on the likelihood of demand being price inelastic for food products would also be valid.

(ii) Further evidence of government failure is shown in the fifth and sixth paragraphs of the extract. Farmers receive less than one third of the CAP payments made by the government and consumers. Administrators have to be paid, along with the surplus stock and storage agencies. Farmers who export their products outside the EU also have to be paid compensation. This is the difference between the guaranteed minimum price and the lower world price of products.

It is also ridiculous for the government to pay farmers to produce surplus goods which are not wanted. The farmers are also using up more factor inputs such as land, labour, machinery and fertiliser that could be reallocated to better use in other industries. It represents a real misallocation of resources.

Finally, just 20% of farmers receive 80% of total subsidies, suggesting that the CAP is an unfair method of intervention. It appears that the large farmers who produce grain benefit far more than the small farmers who produce livestock. Government intervention might be regarded as inefficient here since the large farmers are likely to remain in production without the subsidies.

6/6 marks

e This is an excellent answer in which the candidate examines three separate government failures. Full marks would be awarded either to two points which were really well developed or three points developed reasonably well. Another government failure to which the candidate could have referred is the high tariff barriers imposed on agricultural imports from outside the EU. This could have serious consequences for developing countries which have a comparative advantage in certain cash crops, such as citrus fruits, olives, maize and sorghum. Import controls restrict competition, encourage inefficiency and may lead to retaliatory action.

(c) (i) Government spending on agriculture is increasing in absolute terms but decreasing as a percentage of total government expenditure. This is possible as long as total government spending is increasing overall — the two factors can be reconciled. **2/4 marks**

e The candidate is correct but has failed to use the data from the graphs.

(ii) Without reform of the CAP it will be extremely hard to enlarge the EU. Many of the countries which have applied to join have large agricultural sectors, for example Poland and Hungary. There are possibly millions of small farmers who would qualify for agricultural subsidies. However, the European Commission does not have the money to pay for these subsidies and would risk bankruptcy. Consequently, reform is necessary. It might be that new members would have

a qualifying period before they become eligible for grants and by this time the grants could be phased out.   **4/4 marks**

e A good answer in which the candidate expands on ideas from the extract.

(d) The proposed agricultural reforms are likely to reduce incomes of large farmers as subsidy payments to them will be capped. In addition, since they produce the biggest surpluses they have most to lose when the guaranteed price system is scrapped. European consumers could gain through lower food prices and more choice.

The European Commission's financial position is likely to improve. The downward trend shown in Figure 1 is likely to continue as it saves a lot of money. Some of the funds are likely to be switched to improving the quality of wildlife in the countryside but money could still be left over to spend on other areas, for example, manufacturing industry in depressed regions.   **6/12 marks**

e It is important to note the three parts to this question, namely, the impact of reform for farmers, consumers and the government. The examiner's mark scheme allocates 4 marks for each part.

To earn more marks the candidate could mention how small farmers may gain from the proposed changes. This is mentioned clearly in the text. Farmers may end up being paid a lump sum for looking after the countryside, unrelated to production levels.

The candidate also needs to expand the effects on consumers. For example, consumer choice is likely to increase through removing agricultural trade barriers; the increase in international competition is likely to reduce prices, as some overseas producers are highly efficient. Other ideas could also be raised here, e.g. the prospect of importing genetically modified food from the USA or the elimination of food stockpiles leading to shortages in times of poor harvest.

The candidate grasps the idea that EU government finances are likely to improve and makes reference to data in the graph.

Scored 24/40 = grade C